A TREASURE TROVE OF WISDOM

Collectibles for the mind and soul

Deeptaketuu Chaatterjee

A Treasure Trove of Wisdom

Copyright © 2025 Deeptaketuu Chaatterjee

All rights reserved. No part of this book may be reproduced, stored in a retrieval system, or transmitted in any form or by any means, electronic, mechanical, photocopying, recording, or otherwise, without the prior written permission of the author.

This book is sold as is, without any warranties, express or implied. The author and publisher are not responsible for any problems that may arise from using this book. If you have a problem with the book, your only option is to return it for a refund. The author agrees to protect the publisher from any legal issues that may arise from the book's content. Any legal disputes about this book will be handled according to the laws of the constitution of India

Publisher: Inkscribe Publishing Pvt. Ltd.

ISBN Number: 978-1-966421-88-7

CONTENTS

	Introduction	5
1.	The Miracles Of The Mind	9
2.	Mastering Procrastination: 5 Signs And Timeless Triumph	18
3.	Taming The Inner Demons	24
4.	Managing Stress—The Scriptural Way	33
5.	Resist Resistance, Break The Shackles!	39
6.	Just Breathe!	46
7.	Listening—That's Such A Waste Of Time!	52
8.	A Joyous Journey Called *Life*	59
9.	Love Yourself, But How?	67
10.	5 Life-Changing Quotes Of Eckhart Tolle	72
11.	Sachin, The Modern-Day Arjuna	78
12.	Easter – A Time For Inner Resurrection	83
13.	This Too Shall Pass	88
14.	Are The Eightfold Paths Of Buddhism Passé?	93
15.	Some Spine-Chilling Words Of The Swami	101
16.	What If You Can't 'Let Go'?	106
17.	It's All In The Balance, Or Is It?	112
18.	Success Is A Journey, Not A Destination	122

INTRODUCTION

So, how did it all start?

Well, one afternoon while at work, I got a call from my wife. "Can we consider immigrating to Canada?" Exactly the question that I was contemplating asking her, as I was inundated with calls from immigration agencies, promising a great life abroad—something that could radically transform the lives of our two children, apart from the career growth and abundance it could bring—in summary, a life that we couldn't realistically envisage in India.

To cut a long story short, the dream destination eluded us; not only that, but the pursuit also turned our lives upside down. I quit my job, COVID struck, financial crisis ensued—in short, life became a living hell.

That's when I started looking deep within—were there answers lying inside when the outside world seemed to be in shambles?

A lot (some would say, ALL) of the answers that we seek are hidden in the enlightening discourse of our scriptures (irrespective of the religion you follow). To add to this, saintly philosophers like Ramakrishna Paramahamsa, Swami Vivekananda, Aristotle, Marcus Aurelius, etc., along with modern-day spiritual and self-help gurus like Tony Robbins, Abraham Hicks, Mel Robbins, Gaur Gopal Das, Eckhart Tolle, James Clear, and more, have allowed me to look at life from a different lens. A more reflective take on life.

As I started exploring their works, my first book, 'Fakeism' (inspired heavily by Rhonda Byrne, Joseph Murphy, and Napoleon Hill), seemed to take shape on its own—it was the first step in discovering my Ikigai and then following it.

Introduction

It opened up a new dimension for me—a career as a writer. While it didn't quite go the way I had intended, I could work my way up the freelancing ladder as a content writer. Most importantly, what it meant was I needn't go back to the corporate rat race, which I had vowed not to return to.

But then, what happened to my 'Why' of taking up writing as a vocation? After all, tech content creation was not my only goal.

I embarked on this journey so that I could help my readers navigate some of the difficult phases in life that I had to overcome.

Despite the challenges of a new profession, I did find time to create some blogs on mindful living.

A chance discussion with my cousin sparked the idea of compiling them into a book that could reach a different set of readers.

Thus, I present to you 'A Treasure Trove of Wisdom'!

It's my personal tryst with spiritual learnings from the Holy Bible, the Bhagavad Gita, and the works of deep thinkers like Swami Vivekananda, Aristotle, and Eckhart Tolle, to name a few. I've also lent some scientific validation that may appeal to readers who look for research-based evidence.

The practices and perspectives presented in this context are not meant to serve as professional or spiritual recommendations. These practices have proven effective for me, aiding in the quest for clarity, resilience, and a more profound sense of purpose during difficult periods.

However, I must warn you against repetitive concepts like mindfulness, meditation, procrastination and so forth. The fact that these topics keep cropping up is in itself testimony to the significance they hold in our lives. Whether you are trying to break the shackles of resistance or getting rid of habitual procrastination, or simply starting your spiritual journey, the core elements of mindful living will help you at every step.

Having said that, I've tried to add different perspectives to these recurring theories, and you may find some more relevant than others in your specific state of mind. Hence, readers are invited to engage with this content thoughtfully and to modify or dismiss any concepts as they deem appropriate.

This is ultimately an invitation for you to reflect, experiment, and navigate your own journey towards greater self-awareness, rather than a set of instructions to follow.

Happy reading, and happy living!

THE MIRACLES OF THE MIND

EXPLORING NEUROPLASTICITY: THE SCIENCE BEHIND THE "POWER OF THE MIND"

"You have power over your mind—not outside events. Realise this and you will find strength."—Marcus Aurelius. Where from does this 'magician-mind' find its immense potency? Let's find out…

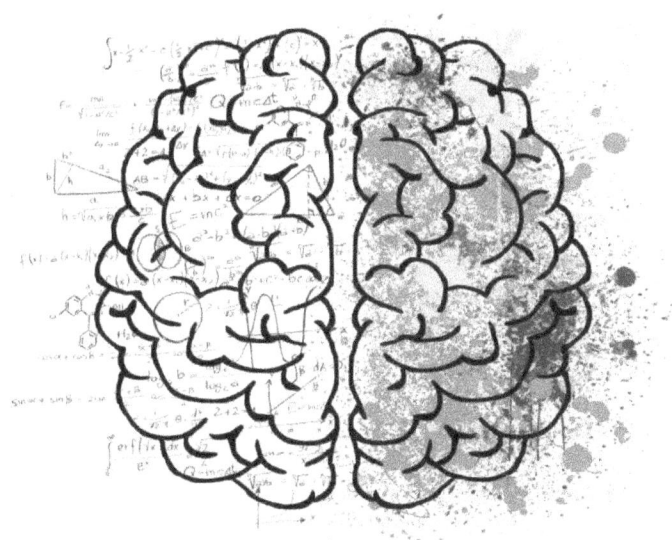

Image by Elisa Riva (pixabay.com)

Mental trauma and its ramifications are not a new phenomenon. It has affected generations and wreaked havoc on many families. However, in the last few years or so, the internet has become inundated with reports of mental degeneration and a variety of mental illnesses.

The Covid Cauldron

When the pandemic broke out in early 2020, the predominant news around the disease focused on the physical damage that the virus could cause. As we became more aware of the dos and don'ts during the COVID-19 outbreak, the mental consequences of the deadly disease began to sink in.

The caged body also led to a trapped mind within the boundaries of our homes. With less intellectual stimulation, the mind began to play tricks. Uncertainties about the future, unexpected and often huge financial hits, and the loss of loved ones all worked together to attack the mind, leading to an alarming rise in mental afflictions. Depression, suicidal tendencies, anger, and temperamental issues began to emerge all over the world.

The situation also gave birth to a new crop of "mental gurus," or people claiming expertise in dealing with the mind and its latent powers.

Popularised several decades ago by proponents of the Law of Attraction, this game of the mind has found many takers on social media.

Mindfulness, meditation, pranayama, affirmations, visualisation, and other techniques intended to unleash the immense power of the mind have since gained increased popularity and acceptance.

Nevertheless, one wonders: are these mere jargons? Or worse still, are these just money-minting marketing gimmicks? Is there a scientific basis for the claimed potency of the mind to reshape our lives?

Well, an answer to these compelling questions could be found in the following discourse.

So let's dive into it!

Our Thoughts And Our Minds

The philosophy around the "power of the mind" hinges on the concept of our thoughts influencing the outcomes of our lives. It suggests that the mind can be trained, shaped, and modified to change our lives in ways we have never imagined before.

The scientific study of the behavioural patterns of our brain's neurons bears an intriguing resemblance to the age-old concept of "mind power."

The mental maze called the brain

Image by vecstock on Freepik

The human brain is largely believed to contain around 100 billion neurons (though more recent studies suggest different estimates), and each neuron can make up to 10,000 connections with other neurons.

What a mindblowing example of interconnectedness! So, what happens next?

These connections, called synapses, send electrical signals. They act as transmitters between the neurons to send and receive information.

Our brains start out very malleable when we're born, and they remain that way for the first few years of life, after which they become less flexible. The human brain can generate new neurons throughout a person's lifetime, but this ability declines with age. In the regular course of life, an average person loses between 10 and 20 percent of their brain cells as they age.

Neuroplasticity- the scientific endeavour to unravel the mysteries of the brain

The brain's ability to change and adapt in response to experience and/or injury over a person's life span is called "neuroplasticity." It happens in response to new experiences, thoughts, emotions, the environment, or sensory input. It is a complex process that happens in all of us and is necessary for learning, memorising new things, and healing injured or diseased tissues or organs. Learning, thinking, creating, and imagining are just some of the acts that activate the brain, which in turn strengthens connections between existing neurons and creates new ones.

Ways in which Neuroplasticity can enhance the brain's capacity

In recent years, the concept of neuroplasticity has become more popular, and it is being studied to see if it can help treat a number of disorders, such as addiction, anxiety, depression, dyslexia, chronic pain, obsessive-compulsive disorder, post-traumatic stress disorder, and schizophrenia.

Wow! That's a lot of work. No wonder everyone goes gaga over brain power. Well, is there more in store?

Neuroplasticity has the potential to alter our perceptions of ageing and cognitive decline because it suggests that the brain continues to grow and change throughout our lives.

It allows us to learn new skills and pick up new hobbies more easily. It can help older adults recover more quickly after a head injury or stroke. Neuroplasticity can further help us improve our response to therapy, especially when it comes to treating anxiety, depression, and substance use disorders.

It can improve processing speed, attention span, and memory capacity.

While it's an ongoing study, neuroscientists have made significant progress in validating past claims about the regenerative capacity of the human brain.

When did the study of neuroplasticity gain momentum?

The American philosopher and psychologist William James first used the term "plasticity" in the context of behavioural science in 1890 in his book "The Principles of Psychology." His idea that the brain and its functionalities are not static in adulthood was largely ignored until relatively recent times.

As the Spanish writer-philosopher Baltasar Gracian said, "The wise does at once what the fool does at last." (pun intended)

The first scientific evidence of brain plasticity was found in a 1964 research paper by American scientist Marian Cleeves Diamond. Marian

Diamond, one of the pioneers of modern neuroscience, did some of her most important research on Albert Einstein's brain to find out what glial cells do in the brain. Paul Bach-y-Rita, Michael Merzenich, and Jon Kass are other prominent figures who helped bring out vital facts to corroborate this amazing prowess of the human brain.

While pages can be filled with the profound and most arduous work carried out by several scientists over the years, the question that lingers on is:

How did men stimulate the brain centuries ago, even before the birth of modern science?

Brain power, the Buddhist way

The teachings of Gautama Buddha are life-long studies in themselves and mandate a separate discourse to milk the cream of Buddhism.

However, we can ponder for a while the impact of one aspect of Buddhist life on our brains: the potency of meditation. We have a separate piece that dives deeper… but let's scratch the surface a bit.

Dr. Richard Davidson, William James and Vilas Professor of Psychology and Psychiatry at the University of Wisconsin–Madison and Founder Director of the "Center for Healthy Minds," has conducted extensive studies on the brainwaves of Buddhist monks.

His experiential research has revealed mind-boggling facts about the supreme prowess of the brains of Olympic-level meditators (with more than 10,000 hours of meditation).

Are you kidding me? 10,000 hours of meditation!

A French-born monk named Mattie Ricard from the Shechen Monastery was asked to meditate on "unconditional loving-kindness and compassion," while scientists monitored his brain's reaction through sophisticated mechanisms. The result was an astounding activity of gamma rays: his brain waves vibrated at 40 cycles per second, indicating intense focus.

To further validate the outcome, other monks were invited to Dr. Davidson's laboratory in Wisconsin. They produced 30 times more gamma rays than a group of college students who were observed at the same time.

The in-depth research clearly showcases the way the human brain can be tuned to produce reactions based on lifestyle, thoughts, and environmental influences.

The potency of Vedic learning

Studies of the Vedas and their method of learning have a profound influence on our mental aptitude. It has been used since ancient times to enhance mental clarity, concentration, and creativity. Through Vedic practises such as meditation and yoga, we can gain access to our inner wisdom and use it to create a better life for ourselves.

Image by Freepik

Scriptural knowledge now gets scientific validation.

A study conducted by the Centre for Biomedical Research, Lucknow, India, showcased the tremendous impact of Vedic learning on enhancing the performance of our brains. With the help of the magnetic resonance imaging (MRI) technique, the research was carried out on 25 Vedic scholars and compared with proficient Sanskrit speakers who were not trained in Vedic literature. A three-layered analysis was conducted that included measuring the grey and white matter of the brain, calculating the brain's thickness, and evaluating the brain's surface structure.

The revelations reinforce the impact of sacred literature on defining the brain's performance matrix.

Vedic learning methods were proven to help enhance the "grey matter" in the thalamus, midbrain, middle frontal brain, angular gyrus, pons, and medulla. They augment our gross motor skills, visual and auditory input processing abilities, concentration and memory, and even respiratory capacities.

With increased brain thickness in the temporal poles, the Vedic scholars demonstrated stronger socio-emotional skills. The increased surface structure also enriched their articulation and oratory abilities.

The continuum

The fascinating study of the human brain and its evolution is an endless topic for discussion. It opens up the seemingly infinite possibilities that are hidden within each of us. By altering our conditioned minds and the thought process that has been imbibed in us since childhood, we usher in opportunities to radically transform our lives. Sceptics would be there to challenge the authenticity of such claims, but that should propel us to continue our quest to demystify the powers of the brain.

Our scriptures have always portrayed the immense capabilities of the brain or mind.

According to yogic traditions, Lord Shiva is considered the first yogi or the Adiyogi. About 15000 years ago, the Adiyogi is believed to have said that we can use the brain's existing capacity much more effectively by becoming more physically and mentally conscious.

To conclude, the Bible says, "For who has the mind of the Lord so as to instruct him? But we have the mind of Christ." (1 Corinthians 2.16).

MASTERING PROCRASTINATION: 5 SIGNS AND TIMELESS TRIUMPH

PROGRESS IS ON THE OTHER SIDE OF PROCRASTINATION

Unlock Your Potential and Defy the Chains of Procrastination

Have you felt frustrated at not achieving your true potential? Have you experienced that nagging feeling that you could have done more with your life? Quite often, in these situations, you end up blaming your circumstances, past or present, as the sole culprit for pushing your life in a direction that you didn't choose. However, honest introspection would reveal that life had given you the opportunity to follow your dreams, but you were not up for the challenge. You kept waiting for the "right time," and even if that ever-elusive "right time" did arrive, you were too lazy to take action.

The shackles of procrastination have been a barrier to self-realisation for ages. From Vedic seers to modern philosophers to successful athletes and businessmen, all have striven to draw our attention to the restrictive nature of procrastination.

Let us explore this subject in greater detail.

What is Procrastination?

In common parlance, procrastination is the act of delaying or postponing tasks that generally merit your attention. It's an insidious enemy that wears the mask of relaxation while chipping away at your capacity for achievement. Resistance or fear are the catalysts that enhance the potency of procrastination. According to Proverbs 10:4, the Bible warns against sloth and stresses the significance of hard work, "Lazy hands make for poverty, but diligent hands bring wealth."

In What Ways Do Procrastination Impair Your Progress?

Procrastination is a severe impediment to forward progress. It creates a vicious circle of missed chances, reduced production, and diminished self-confidence. A revered scripture, the Bhagavad Gita, exhorts you to execute your obligations with unwavering focus, releasing attachment to outcomes. According to Bhagavad Gita 18:28, "The one who is in the state of ignorance is the one who is undisciplined, vulgar, stubborn, deceitful, slothful, despondent, and a procrastinator." When we give in to procrastination, we get caught up in the bonds of attachment, which slow us down on the path to enlightenment.

Five Tell-Tale Signs of Procrastination:

1. **Task Avoidance:** Avoiding critical tasks by indulging in trivial or insignificant activities.

How often have Netflix or Amazon Prime overtaken the need to pursue a side hustle that can change your life? Or that online course that can give you the edge over your peers?

2. **Excuse Creation:** Relying on elaborate excuses to justify delays and rationalise inaction.

The cloudy morning has so frequently put you off going to the gym. Instead of using the home treadmill, you have convinced yourself that you need your instructor to monitor your progress and have waited for the perfect day to hit the gym.

3. **Perfectionism Paralysis:** Getting stuck in an endless pursuit of perfection, leading to prolonged delays.

Haven't you told yourself, "Let the family wedding get over; I will surely start my keto diet?" Many resolutions die a natural death waiting for the New Year to arrive.

4. **Delaying Decision:** Postponing decisions due to fear of making the wrong choice results in missed opportunities.

Isn't it common to find people stuck in an unprogressive career but still waiting for the next appraisal to turn things around instead of pursuing a new job or career opportunity?

5. **Time Mismanagement:** Habitually overestimating the time required for tasks and failing to prioritise effectively.

"Oh, tidying up the living room will take the whole day; let's do it next week." Doesn't the statement sound familiar?

The Detrimental Effects of Procrastination:

1. **Diminished Productivity:** Procrastination hampers our ability to accomplish tasks efficiently and meet deadlines, leading to subpar results.

2. **Increased Stress and Anxiety:** Procrastination creates a mounting sense of pressure and stress as tasks pile up and deadlines loom closer.

3. **Missed Opportunities:** By postponing tasks, we risk missing valuable opportunities for growth, learning, and advancement.

4. **Damaged Self-Confidence:** Procrastination undermines our self-belief and erodes our confidence, making it harder to achieve our goals.

5. **Strained Relationships:** Procrastination can cause frustration and strain in relationships when it leads to unmet commitments or unfulfilled promises.

A Five-Step Formula to Overcome Procrastination:

1. Self-Reflection: Engage in introspection to understand the underlying reasons for your procrastination tendencies. Explore your fears, insecurities, and self-imposed limitations.

Breaking the shackles takes immense mental resolve, but once you experience the freedom of self-expression, no goal will seem unattainable.

Like the great Khalil Gibran said, *"You may chain my hands, you may shackle my feet; you may even throw me into a dark prison; but you shall not enslave my thinking, because it is free!"*

2. Set Clear Goals: Establish specific, achievable goals, breaking them down into manageable steps. This clarity provides a sense of direction and minimizes overwhelm.

The Law of Attraction promotes the technique of visualisation. There are great exponents of this philosophy who have even invoked the curiosity of the scientific world. However, so many people fail in their initial quest to visualise and manifest their deepest desires. Ever wondered why?

Take a cue from this YouTube video of Mel Robbins, the famous motivational speaker, author, and podcast host, https://www.youtube.com/watch?v=qIpk4oh9Zak. Try breaking your visualisation process into a series of small steps. If you are procrastinating on your health goals, visualise sweating it out in the gym every day, imagine the pain, and eventually the joy of overcoming those barriers to achieve your dream physique. By breaking it down into achievable steps, you tune your mind into believing that the desired outcome is possible. You also start taking action to move toward your goals rather than spending meaningless hours in wishful thinking.

3. Cultivate Discipline: Foster self-discipline through consistent practice and dedication. Embrace small, consistent actions that propel you forward, despite any internal resistance.

In the words of one of the most influential motivational speakers, Jim Rohn, "Discipline is the bridge between goals and accomplishment."

4. Practice Mindfulness: Cultivate present-moment awareness to recognize when procrastination tendencies arise. Mindfulness empowers us to choose proactive actions aligned with our long-term objectives.

Our minds work overtime to generate a plethora of thoughts at every moment. It's natural to get caught up in useless thinking that promotes inaction. In the middle of preparing that important pitch presentation for potential investors, you may drift off to the dream of launching your 100th restaurant in the heart of Manhattan. While science-backed manifestation techniques may help you achieve your dream, you need to be in the present moment to nail that all-important business meeting.

5. Seek Support: Surround yourself with a supportive network of friends, mentors, or accountability partners who can offer encouragement, guidance, and gentle reminders along your journey.

We all stumble at some stage in our quest to keep moving toward our goals. A rainy day may tempt the athlete to take an unscheduled break. On such days, it helps if your training partner shares a video of a short, high-intensity workout session at home. You are likely to get charged to hit the treadmill yourself.

Procrastination has robbed the world of several gems. So many talented individuals have been lost in the crowd because they didn't take life by the scruff of their neck and channel it in the right direction. Science indicates that procrastination is a habit, like waking up late or eating too much junk food. Like all negative habits, you nurture them and transform them into giants that end up devouring your lives. Instead, take note of the warning signs of procrastination and act to navigate past the hurdles that they present.

The holy books of the world and the sterling work of many great thinkers are your eternal guides.

TAMING THE INNER DEMONS

HOW DO YOU WIN THE WAR OF THE MIND?

Arjuna says in the Bhagavad Gita, *"The mind is very restless, turbulent, strong and obstinate, O Krishna. It appears to me that it is more difficult to control than the wind."* - **BG:6.34**

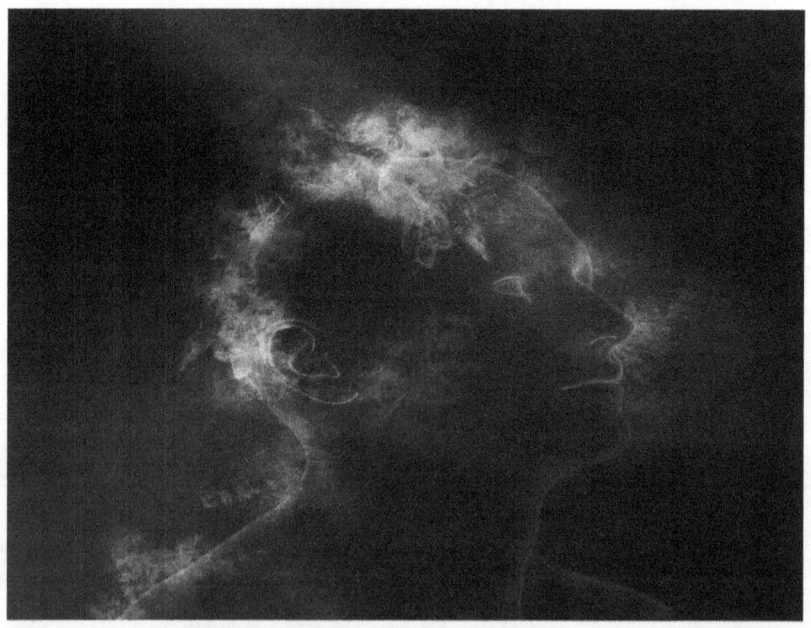

Image by kjpargeter on Freepik

Lord Krishna acknowledges the tumultuous nature of the mind- *"...the mind is indeed very difficult to restrain."* - BG:6.35. He later goes on to explain how we can tame the turbulent mind, which we will look at later in the piece.

The mind can shelter both the holy spirit and the demon. In order to break free from the oppressive clutches of the latter, we first need to identify the traits that turn our minds into battlefields.

Come, let's say hello (from a distance) to some of them!

Fear: Can safely be termed the leader of the pack, fear manifests itself in broadly two forms: physical and psychological. To break them into tangible points, let's dive into each of them separately.

- **Physical fear:** Mortal fear, or a fear of probable physical harm, is often an instinctive reaction.

  Imagine you are at the dead end of a dark alley, with goons wielding deadly weapons and threatening to pounce on you. It would send a chill down your spine.

  In a more realistic situation, even crossing a highway with cars and heavy vehicles whizzing past at a rate of knots could be nerve-wracking.

  However, these fear factors are natural and usually help us avoid real-life dangers. As such, they are not harmful since specific circumstances trigger them.

- **Psychological fear:** This is the killer one and can cloud our minds in so many ways. While mental or psychological fear can be a separate topic of discussion, let's look at two aspects that restrain us from living the lives of our dreams- a) fear of failure, and b) fear of missing out (FOMO).

- **Fear of failure:** Remember the childhood dream of starting your own cafe or a music academy?

Even if you make the best coffee and sandwiches in your locality and your friends keep telling you, "Mate, it's about time you started your own venture," you haven't done that.

Maybe while sipping a cup of freshly brewed Arabica on your couch, looking listlessly through the window pane at the drizzling downpour, you still imagine your cafe bustling with customers on a rainy afternoon.

While several practical predicaments stop us from taking the plunge, our inhibitions often bind us to the mundane life that we internally crave to break free from.

"What if you fail?"

"What if you lose all your savings and run into debt?"

"What will society say?"

... these incessant questions keep clamouring in our minds

- **Fear of missing out:** This has become a talking point since we have become social media freaks.

Oh, the lovely pictures of the scenic Santorini or the dazzling designer outfit to go with the latest model of Lexus that your peers and relatives may have experienced or bought are all over social media.

They raise the bar of your material desires. We keep comparing our apparently miserable lives with those of our friends, neighbours, and colleagues.

We feel like slogging harder to earn the extra buck.

This never-ending rat race takes us miles away from our deepest desires.

- **Anger:** A close challenger for the number one spot, anger is the other demon that keeps us cocooned in a world of despair and frustration. It usually stems from a blaming mindset where we try to blame external factors for whatever is going on in our lives.

You are annoyed at not getting the promotion that you felt you deserved. You blame your boss or your peers for manipulating the appraisal.

You are angry that the house is a mess every time you come back from work. You blame your spouse or the children for not tidying up.

You are freaked out that your son didn't score more than the neighbour's daughter. "Why didn't you prepare harder?" you scream at your son.

You are mad at getting a ticket while rushing to the office in the morning madness. "I crossed before it turned red. Wish I had the time to take you to court, you moron," you mentally curse the traffic guard.

-and the list goes on.

- **Procrastination:** You can call it the silent killer. It creeps up almost imperceptibly and covers our lives like a rash.

You won't join the gym as you are perennially waiting for the "right time." Remember the New Year resolution you made back in 2019?

Your dream book still remains a dream since the "Sunday" you plan to start writing never arrives.

The half-baked business plan was shelved long ago, as you are waiting for the markets to stabilise, for your kids to finish high school, and for your savings to reach X amount before you revisit the venture of your dream that once kept you awake all night.

There are other miscreants like lust, jealousy, suffering (which is nothing but unavoidable pain turned into lifelong misery), and more.

However, if you can tackle the three main devils, then you will move towards the light of life that beckons you all the time- and it's not a mirage; it's real and vibrant.

So, how do we tame our inner demons?

Image by pikisuperstar on Freepik

These vagaries of the mind are an inevitable fallout of the stressful life that we endure.

Hence, the first step is to accept that you will encounter them at some point in your life. You have to be resolute in the battle with your own idiosyncrasies.

Let's handle each of them separately.

Fighting Fear

As we have discussed before, genuine mortal fear is not necessarily harmful; hence, we will move on to the other manifestations of fear.

For the sake of clarity, we had segregated the two into fear of failure and fear of mission out.

However, there's a common thread.

In both cases, the main culprit is our fear of being judged. We are scared that if we fail, our society, friends, relatives, and maybe even our immediate family will mark us as incompetent.

Here are some tips to combat fear:

- **Relive your victories:** Every time you are afraid of failing, think about the moments you succeeded. It could be the relay race in school, the college extempore, or something more recent at work, like cracking an improbable deal.

Recall how your friends cheered for you, how you made your parents proud as you stood on the winners' podium, and the pat on the back from your boss.

These happy memories will rekindle your sense of self-belief. If you have done it in the past, you can jolly well do it again.

- **You are your biggest challenger and critic:** Strive to become a better version of yourself every day.

You are the only one who has the birthright to judge yourself; others can share their views (and often they open up new perspectives), so listen to them.

But don't allow external views to change your perception of yourself.

This approach also negates the impact of FOMO. You are no longer bothered by your peer group's success.

The focus shifts from the external world to your internal realms.

While you don't want to become self-obsessed, you divert your attention to self-improvement and self-care.

📌 **Plan, prepare, and plunge:** While following your gut feeling usually leads to the right path, you don't want to be reckless.

- Plan what you intend to do
- Prepare properly for the tasks ahead. This may mean acquiring new skills before embarking on a new venture
- Take the plunge with a sustainable base of 6-8 months

This takes care of your anxieties about starting something new or following your chosen path.

Accelerating Anger Management

"......But through practise and detachment, it can be controlled."- B.G: 6.35

Taking a cue from this guidance from Lord Krishna in the Bhagavad Gita, you can try the following steps to counter anger:

📌 **Practice mindfulness:** A few deep breaths, a relaxed mind, and a deliberate focus on the tasks at hand are the best ways to quieten the whirlwind that threatens to blow things away.

There are several types of mindfulness and meditation practices that will help you with anger management. Try the following process to begin with:

- Sit in a comfortable position with your back relaxed but erect.

- Take three deep breaths
- Start counting slowly from 10-1 backwards
- Keep reminding yourself that you are gradually relaxing, both physically and mentally

This short exercise helps your mind move from the beta state to the alpha state.

When anxiety strikes, try moving to the Alpha or the Gamma state of mind for relaxed attention or deep concentration.

🔸 **Take ownership:** The moment the mind tells you that someone else is responsible for something that's affecting your life, tell it to "Shut up! It's my life, and I take complete ownership of whatever is happening in it."

In reality, everything is not in your control. But by refraining from the blame game, you give yourself a chance to reflect.

That's when you'll find most of the answers.

You'll emerge more competent and confident to take actions that define the outcomes.

🔸 **Gratitude journaling:** One of the best ways to stop fretting over what you don't have is to be thankful for what you have.

- Before you retire to bed, practise writing down five good things that happened to you that day.
- Also, write five good deeds that you did during the day.

Even if they seem trivial, give it a try. What matters is diverting your mind to the "haves" from "have-nots".

Postponing Procrastination

As life-transforming, best-selling author James Clear says, "The seed of every habit is a single tiny decision."

We often procrastinate when the entire picture seems overwhelming.

- Break into small, actionable parts
- Inculcate a habit-forming mindset rather than a goal-setting one
- Visualise the process of achieving your goals as opposed to the end goals. As you move forward in your journey, you can modify the scene.

Get up and get moving. A beautiful life awaits you on the other side.

Final Words

In this dynamic world of constant change, what will keep us grounded and aligned with our life's mission is a steady mind.

If you can't get rid of the inner demons, then at least keep them tightly leashed.

Image by Freepik

Your mind's battlefield will metamorphose into a happy playground.

'It is only when man tames his own demons that he becomes the king of himself, if not the world.'- Joseph Campbell

MANAGING STRESS—THE SCRIPTURAL WAY

HOW TO MANAGE STRESS: THE HOLY BIBLE SHOWS THE PATH!

Head in your hands, drooping shoulders, dreary eyes, and a cry from within: "When will this end?"

Image by Nik Shuliahin (Unsplash.com)

STRESS manifests itself in myriad ways. A word that has become part and parcel of modern life… a word that is so loosely used that it may have lost its lethal impact. But the effects are something that you can't run away from.

The American Psychological Association states that more than a quarter of adult Americans are so stressed that they find it difficult to function normally.

However, a large percentage of the affected populace is in denial mode. It's a defence mechanism that allows them to turn a blind eye to what has become an obvious problem.

The Austrian neurologist Sigmund Freud, who is often called the "father of modern psychology," popularised the concept of "denial." The pioneer of psychoanalysis, Sigmund Freud, reckoned that the defence mechanism is used as an anxiety deterrent. People in this mode deny that any mental problems, like memories, feelings, or thoughts, exist.

Still, the urge to reach out for help comes up every once in a while, even though it is often pushed down out of fear of being judged by society.

Image by Nikko Macaspac (Unsplash.com)

Where, then, must you turn for refuge? Where do you seek shelter from the downpour that threatens to drown you in an abyss of hopelessness?

The Lord had sent his beloved son as the saviour. And in his words, you can find the elixir of life, which is the power to stop this overwhelming feeling from engulfing you completely.

Body basics

"Do you not know that your body is a temple of the Holy Spirit within you, which you have from God? …. So glorify God in your body." (1 Corinthians 6: 19,20)

This power statement from the holy book of Christianity implies that you must pay heed to your body, the abode that cocoons the presence of the higher spirits within you.

So how do you maintain this temple? A few simple habits, if inculcated in your daily routine, can produce wondrous results:

- Exercise to help your body fight stress

Exercising regularly has many health benefits, but it can be even more beneficial when you're under stress. Stressed muscles tend to feel more tense and tight, which can lead to back and joint pain. Exercising regularly, including cardio and strength training, helps your body relax. This can reduce the risk of injury and help you cope better with stress.

- Maintain a balanced, and healthy diet

As the old saying goes, "You are what you eat." In essence, this means that your diet influences cell structure, hormones, and neurotransmitters. A healthy diet with a balanced proportion of carbohydrates, protein, vitamins, and minerals keeps the body (remember, the temple) in shape.

- Get adequate sleep

According to Dr. Michael Twery, a sleep expert at the National Institute of Health, sleep is not only essential for the brain but also for our immune system, appetite, blood pressure, and cardiovascular health, among other things. Lack of sleep can lead to obesity and heart disease. There's a strong correlation between melatonin (sleep hormones) and cortisol levels (stress hormones). Irregular sleeping patterns can disturb the intended functioning of the respective hormones.

Take a break

"Six days you shall do your work, but on the seventh day you shall rest"
(Exodus 23: 12)

In the hustle culture of modern times, you may not be able to follow the commandment to a T, but you must set aside time for complete rest. It may not be a Sunday; it may not even be one whole day, but a part thereof, which you will allocate for resting and rejuvenating. This could also be the time you allow divine presence to heal you, both physically and emotionally.

If you find yourself overwhelmed by your stress or overwhelmed by a particular stressor, try to take a break. This doesn't mean you need to stop trying to solve the problem; it just means that you need a break from it. Ideally, you can take a few minutes, leave the stressors alone, and come back to them when you're feeling better.

Calmness is a habit, developed through spiritual practice

"Have no anxieties about anything, but in everything by prayer and supplication with thanksgiving let your requests be made known to God. And the peace of God, which passes all understanding, will keep your hearts and minds in Christ Jesus." (Philippians 4: 6,7)

To a troubled mind, this may seem superficial, but with dedicated spiritual practice, you can make peace with the demons in your mind.

What's more, even scientific research has revealed the impact of some such methods. Let's explore some of them.

- The breath of all things

There are many ways to control how we breathe, which has long-lasting effects on our physical, mental, and emotional health. Breathwork also called breathing therapies, has its roots in Eastern practices like yoga and tai chi, among others. Over the years, Western psychotherapy techniques have embraced the healing powers of deep breathing.

There are various types of diaphragmatic breathing exercises that can have a physical and mental impact. You can also try the simple practice of taking a deep breath for 5 seconds, holding it for 2 seconds, and releasing it for another 5 seconds. This can regularize your parasympathetic nervous system and help reduce stress and anxiety.

- Guided meditation helps to look within

In the pre-Gen AI era, if you typed "benefits of meditation" on Google, you would have got about 22,70,00,000 results (0.50 seconds). The spiritual and scientific worlds both acknowledge the virtues of this age-old practice.

Commit to such work that has a connection with the Lord

"Let what you say be a simple 'Yes' or 'No'; anything more than this comes from the evil." (Mathew 5: 37)

A major source of our stress comes from our professional endeavours. In our quest to stay ahead in the rat race, we stretch ourselves beyond our limits. And in so doing, we lose sight of the message in our scriptures: "Am I now seeking the favour of men, or of God?.... If I were still pleasing men, I should not be a servant of Christ." (Galatians 1:10)

Work that brings a smile to your face is work meant to serve the Lord.

If you haven't found your "Ikigai" (a Japanese word for your vocation), find time to do something you enjoy. Look for something that you're passionate about and find a way to share that passion with others. This can be done through volunteering, teaching, or mentoring. Getting involved in a community or philanthropy group can also be a great way to relieve stress. Even something as simple as going for a walk or engaging in a creative activity can be a great way to relieve stress.

Practice compassion- it's a stress-buster like none other

"And the Lord's servant must not be quarrelsome but kindly to everyone... correcting his opponents with gentleness....." (2 Timothy 2: 24,25)

When you are stressed out, you tend to be irritable, and ready to take on everyone who contradicts your views.

With mindfulness methods, you can restrict these uncontrolled outbursts. Over time, you can find that lending a shoulder to someone in need or just listening with compassion to their side of the story may actually help you find ways to unburden yourself.

Finally, have faith in the Lord

"Trust in the Lord, and do good; so you will dwell in the land, and enjoy security." (Psalms 37:3)

When all seems dark, close your eyes in prayer... His light always shines for those who seek with the purest of intentions.

RESIST RESISTANCE, BREAK THE
SHACKLES!

TIME FOR ACTION IS RIGHT HERE, RIGHT NOW

When your inner voice comes calling, don't allow "resistance" to play spoilsport.

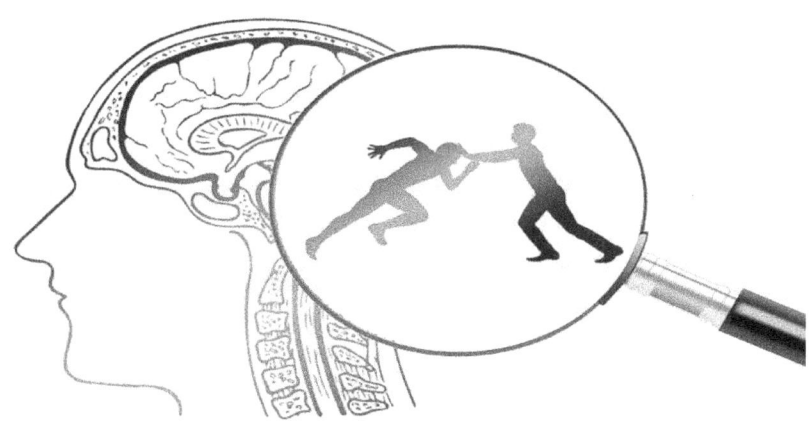

Image by Geralt (Pixabay)

Our minds are conditioned from an early age regarding good and bad, right and wrong, dos and don'ts, and so forth.

As kids, we depend on our parents, grandparents, teachers, and other adults to show us the way. Even though this is mostly necessary until a certain age, we also end up believing the things that are constantly ingrained in our heads.

In typical middle-class families, particularly in the East, it is drilled into our minds that we should be rational in our aspirations and focus on savings more than earnings because the threshold of our earning capacities is almost predefined.

We grow up with a vision of a mundane life that becomes a reality in due course. Remember: "

> *For as he thinks in his heart, so is he." (Proverbs 23:7, New King James Version).*

For some, the prearranged journey leads to a life of fulfilment. Their immaculate academic career naturally progresses to rewarding professional pursuits, punctuated by a happy personal life. However, this picture-perfect life is usually for a privileged few.

For others, our lives can seem like a series of mechanical tasks when we follow the pre-planned path. From the shrill noise of the alarm clock in the morning until slumping down on the bed at midnight or beyond, exhausted both physically and mentally, we become slaves to our own destiny.

A prodigious guitarist sacrifices his passion for survival needs, and the best tennis player in school is convinced by his parents that there's only one Roger Federer in a million: "You won't make the cut, son."

So, we choose to "get grounded," bury our desires, and trudge along the "tried and tested" route that meets the demands of the world.

What happens to our aspirations? What happens to the latent talents we once thought would take us in a totally different direction than where we are now?

We meticulously pack them in boxes and shelve them in the attics of our hearts amidst piles of mental junk.

Image by James Qualtrough (Unsplash)

However, life gives a select few a second chance—a chance to break free and explore the endless possibilities of their dreams and desires.

But taking the road less travelled is a test of one's grit and determination. And on this path, the biggest hurdle is "resistance."

> "Resistance by definition is self-sabotage. But there's a parallel peril that must also be guarded against: sabotage by others." (the WAR of ART by Steven Pressfield)

How does resistance manifest itself in our day-to-day lives?

It's a trickster of the highest order, with a plethora of weapons at its disposal. Let's look at some of them.

- **Fear:** Be it speaking up in just protest against your superior or hitting the publish button for your first article; fear strikes at critical junctures in our lives. The very thought of challenging the status quo or embracing a new beginning sends chills down our spine.

This is the trump card up resistance's sleeve. It freezes us into absolute inaction. We retreat into the mundaneness of a restrained life.

- **Rationalisation:** "If you speak up, your appraisal will be doomed. Just ignore and move on with your job," whispers resistance whenever you try to muster the courage to bring out obvious leadership glitches in your supervisor. "You publish this trash and you'll make a mockery of yourself," warns resistance to keep you from exploring your creative self. To rationalise further, it may add that 'writing' can't be a full-time occupation as "writers struggle to make ends meet."

Resistance uses rationalisation as a complement to fear. The double whammy is usually enough to knock you to your knees.

- **Procrastination:** Ever made a new year resolution of starting a diet or exercise regime? Or just to wake up early for a morning walk? Well, these resolutions often keep getting pushed back by a "few days" that moves to the elusive "next Monday," which then gets thwarted by Monday morning blues.. And the saga continues.

It's resistance at its best. It stops you from taking the steps that can transform you for the better. It strives to nip any well-meant plans in the bud so that you don't experience the fruits of change and cling to the past.

- **Mental afflictions:** This can stir up controversy as clinical depression, anxiety, and other forms of mental ailments are real. However, there's a tendency to equate sadness or laziness with depression. While an actual depressive state may start from a sad incident that can make you less enthusiastic about life, it could be just a passing phase and not a clinical condition.

Resistance has a happy knack for preying on people who proclaim to be depressed at every possible instance. It enjoys keeping you in a state of self-pity so that you don't emerge stronger, more potent, and ready for life's challenges.

- **Victim card:** Acceptance is often the most difficult first step in the process of self-alteration. We love to shove the responsibility on "circumstances", which are supposedly not in our hands. It's true that certain occurrences in our lives are not in our control, but if we introspect honestly, we'll find that we are the creators of the situation we are in. We choose a path that led us to our present circumstances.

Resistance uses the victim card to keep us chained to our current environment. It keeps reminding us of our "responsibilities" that are certain to get derailed if we try to break free.

Resistance gains momentum when your friends and allies, and even your immediate family, start to reinforce its credo.

Two of the most popular pieces of advice we get from our near and dear ones are "play safe" and "it's all destined; you can't change anything." These reaffirmations of our own mental blockages further entrap us in the maze of our minds.

Should you then remain slaves to resistance or show the mettle to break the shackles?

Image by Schaferie (Pixabay)

"I can do all things through Christ who strengthens me" (Philippians 4:13- New King James Version)

Faith in divinity gives us faith in ourselves, as the Holy Spirit resides in us.

Nevertheless, to negate resistance, you need to launch a planned attack. Some of the ammunition in this war is:

- **Planning:** If you want to start a new phase in your life, then plan in advance. It's an obvious safeguard against failures, but more importantly, you can keep resistance at bay if your endeavour is well-planned and not impulsive.
- **Discipline:** Maintain a proper schedule to take action on your plan. If it's about writing, then keep aside a time of the day when you write no matter what (barring medical emergencies, of course). If you are starting a diet plan, will yourself to stay away from the tempting junk food; keep healthy substitutes at hand or

even use distractions like music to keep your mind away from the thoughts.
- **Momentum:** Using the 5–4–3–2–1 technique has worked wonders for me when it comes to setting an early-morning regime or breaking free from writer's block. Just count from 5 to 1 in reverse order and will yourself to start the task. It acts as a jolt that pushes you out of inertia.
- **Persistence:** Resistance is always looking to claw back, and it chooses the difficult days to pounce on you. Remind yourself that everyone has an off day, and be sure to get back to your schedule at the earliest.

In the words of Mark Twain, "Courage is resistance to fear, mastery of fear, not absence of fear."

Hence, be courageous, my friends. Cheers to conquering resistance!

Keep flipping the pages for more.

JUST BREATHE!

AWAKENING INNER HARMONY: HOW MEDITATION TRANSFORMS YOUR LIFE

Harness the Ancient Wisdom of Meditation and Embrace a Transcendent Existence

In the chaotic rhythm of modern life, achieving a sense of inner peace and balance can feel like an unattainable dream. Amidst the clamour of daily obligations, meditation stands as a timeless practice that holds the key to unlocking serenity within ourselves. Rooted in the wisdom of ancient scriptures and validated by modern science, meditation has the potential to revolutionise your life.

Let's explore the profound impact of meditation on mental and physical well-being—citing quotes from the Bhagavad Gita and Buddhism—as well as referencing reputable journals and the words of notable figures.

Join us on this transformative journey and discover the extraordinary power of meditation.

Wisdom from the Scriptures:

The Bhagavad Gita, one of the most revered texts in Hindu philosophy, offers profound insights into meditation. Lord Krishna states, *"A yogi's consciousness, like a lamp in a windless room, does not waver as he meditates on the Supreme." (Bhagavad Gita 6.19).*

Buddhism, too, places equal emphasis on the role of meditation in achieving enlightenment and escaping the cycle of suffering. The Buddha once said, *"Wisdom germinates from meditation; absence of meditation leads to the loss of wisdom" (Dhammapada Verse 282).*

These ancient scriptures guide us towards understanding the importance of stillness and introspection in navigating the complexities of life.

Scientific Validation:

Modern scientific research further reinforces the benefits of meditation, providing tangible evidence for its transformative potential. In a study published in the Journal of Neuroscience, researchers found that meditation can lead to structural changes in the brain, including increased grey matter density in regions associated with attention and emotional regulation (Hölzel et al., 2008).

Furthermore, a meta-analysis published in JAMA Internal Medicine revealed that mindfulness meditation can significantly reduce symptoms of anxiety, depression, and pain (Goyal et al., 2014). The convergence of ancient wisdom and scientific findings solidifies meditation's credibility as a life-changing practice.

Mental Health Benefits:

a) Stress Reduction: Meditation serves as a natural antidote to stress, providing a sanctuary of calmness amidst the chaos of daily life. According to a study published in Frontiers of Psychology, mindfulness meditation can significantly reduce perceived stress and increase work engagement (Bartlett et al., 2021).

b) Improved Emotional Well-Being: Regular meditation enhances emotional resilience and self-awareness. As Jon Kabat-Zinn, a renowned professor of medicine and meditation teacher, states, "You can't stop the waves, but you can learn to surf." Meditation grants us the power to observe and detach from foul thought patterns, thus fostering emotional stability and cultivating a positive outlook on life.

c) Enhanced Concentration: In this world of endless distractions, meditation serves as a potent tool to develop one's focus and enhance concentration. The Dalai Lama once said, "The mind is like a parachute; it works best when it's open." Meditation educates the mind to be in the present, which improves our ability to do things with clarity and efficiency.

d) Boosted Creativity: The hush and calmness of meditation are rich soil for creativity to thrive. Steve Jobs, the co-founder of Apple Inc., attributed his innovative thinking to meditation, stating, "If you just sit and observe, you will see how restless your mind is. If you try to calm it, it only makes it worse. But over time, it does calm, and when it does, there's room to hear more subtle things – that's when your intuition starts to blossom, and you start to see things more clearly and be in the present more. Your mind just slows down, and you see a tremendous expanse in the moment. You see so much more than you could see before. It's a discipline, you have to practice it." (Isaacson, 2011).

e) Increased Mindfulness: Meditation deepens our connection to the present moment, heightening our capacity for mindfulness. According to a study published in the journal Psychological Inquiry, mindfulness meditation enhances attention and awareness, leading to greater engagement and appreciation of life's simple pleasures (Brown et al., 2007).

Physical Health Benefits:

a) Reduced Blood Pressure: Various studies have demonstrated the potency of meditation in reducing blood pressure, thus lowering the risk of cardiovascular disease. In a research review published in the American Journal of Hypertension, meditation was found to have a significant impact on reducing blood pressure levels (Brook et al., 2013).

b) Enhanced Immune System: Regular meditation strengthens the immune system, promoting overall health and well-being. In a study published in the official journal of the American Psychosomatic Society, researchers found that meditation can positively influence the immune response and enhance immune cell activity (Davidson et al., 2003).

c) Improved Sleep: By stilling the mind and easing the body, meditation aids in achieving peaceful sleep, allowing for greater physical restoration and reactivation. The National Sleep Foundation recommends meditation as a valuable tool for improving sleep quality (National Sleep Foundation, 2021).

d) Pain Management: Meditation has been found to reduce chronic pain by altering the perception of pain and enhancing pain tolerance. In a study published in the Journal of Neuroscience, researchers discovered that mindfulness meditation can significantly reduce pain intensity and unpleasantness (Zeidan et al., 2011).

e) Slowed Aging Process: The stress-reducing effects of meditation can slow down cellular ageing, promoting longevity and vitality. Nobel laureate Elizabeth Blackburn, who discovered the role of telomeres in ageing, suggested that engaging in stress-reducing activities, developing positive emotions, and relaxing your mind can preserve your telomeres for longer durations.

Meditation Techniques:

a) Mindfulness Meditation: This method entails paying attention to the here and now and monitoring one's internal experiences, free of judgement. As the Buddha said, "When you realize how perfect everything is, you will tilt your head back and laugh at the sky".

b) Loving-Kindness Meditation: This practise promotes emotional health and connection by encouraging the development of self-love, compassion, and benevolence. In the words of the Dalai Lama, "This is my simple religion. There is no need for temples; no need for complicated philosophy. Our own brain, our own heart is our temple; the philosophy is kindness."

c) Transcendental Meditation: The objective of this approach is to induce a deep state of relaxation and heightened awareness through the repetition of a mantra. As Maharishi Mahesh Yogi, the founder of Transcendental Meditation, stated, "Transcendental Meditation opens the awareness to the infinite reservoir of energy, creativity, and intelligence that lies deep within everyone."

d) Yoga and Meditation: The ancient practice of yoga incorporates physical postures (asanas) with meditation, promoting holistic well-being. Sri Sri Ravi Shankar, a spiritual leader and founder of the Art of Living Foundation, explains, "Yoga is not just exercise and asanas. It is the emotional integration and spiritual elevation with a touch of a mystic element that gives you a glimpse of something beyond all imagination."

In a world fraught with diversions and disunion, meditation does present us with a profound path towards inner concord and transformation. The ageless sagacity of scriptures such as the Bhagavad Gita and Buddhism, coupled with scientific research and the words of eminent personages, bears witness to the wondrous potency of meditation. By embracing regular meditation practice, we can embark on a journey of self-discovery, unlocking the serenity within ourselves and cultivating a life filled with peace, joy, and purpose.

So, take a moment to pause, breathe, and dive into the transformative depths of meditation.

Stir your inner harmony and partake in the paradigm shifts that meditation may bring to your life.

References:

1. https://www.ncbi.nlm.nih.gov/pmc/articles/PMC3004979/
2. https://pubmed.ncbi.nlm.nih.gov/24395196/
3. https://www.frontiersin.org/articles/10.3389/fpsyg.2021.724126/full
4. http://www.gruberpeplab.com/teaching/psych231_fall2013/documents/231_Brown2007.pdf
5. https://www.ahajournals.org/doi/full/10.1161/HYP.0b013e318293645f
6. https://journals.lww.com/psychosomaticmedicine/Abstract/2003/07000/Alterations_in_Brain_and_Immune_Function_Produced.14.aspx
7. https://www.ncbi.nlm.nih.gov/pmc/articles/PMC3090218/

LISTENING—THAT'S SUCH A WASTE OF TIME!

REDISCOVERING THE LOST ART OF LISTENING

Have you ever imagined a world where everyone around you is just talking… relentlessly talking and talking?

Image by Elyas Pasban (Unsplash.com)

Up for a bit of fun?

With your eyes closed, get submerged in a fantasy land where you see every individual just chattering away.

Sounds ridiculous? Try it anyway for a bit of banter.

Welcome back!

Initially, it may have seemed like a hilarious comedy movie, but if you planted yourself in the scene as the sole listener, I bet your head would have started throbbing from the cacophony of noise.

In such a situation, you may catch something interesting here and there, but strain as you might, it would be impossible to make any sense of what's happening around you.

In the midst of the incessant blabbering, sanity will cease to exist. What's worse is that words of wisdom will get swamped in a sea of senseless babble.

Even though the example is a metaphor, you have probably been in similar situations at work or at social events.

Listening in a professional environment

Image by Yan Krukau (Pexels.com)

I remember that in our MBA entrance exam preparations or even during soft skills training in business school, we would undergo several rounds of mock group discussions.

Invariably, there would be a bunch of folks who would jump into the conversation from the word go and would be hard to stop. Some would try to enter the fray with high-pitched voices.

However, the real stars would often exhibit good listening abilities and pounce on a point on which they could elaborate and take the discussion their way.

In corporate meetings, it's not unusual to experience long-lasting monologues. Those are the real testers for people who may have had a late-night party or a hard day's work. You would need multiple doses of caffeine to stay alert (read awake)!

Some people in leadership positions are deeply convinced that lecturing is the best way to get their subordinates to listen to them.

Maybe with them in mind, one of the pioneers of marketing, Peter Drucker, said, "Listening (the first competence of leadership) is not a skill; it is a discipline. All you have to do is keep your mouth shut."

However, we are fortunate not to be surrounded only by such leaders who are readily swayed by their gift of the gab.

True leaders are the ones who have the patience to listen to their teammates, understand their pain points, and then suggest implementable solutions. They are often the leaders of choice who can motivate their teams for bigger and greater achievements.

Listening and empathy

Image by Fauxels (Pexels.com)

The Bible says, "Know this, my beloved brethren. Let every man be quick to hear, slow to speak, slow to anger." (James 1:19)

When you hear with your ears but listen with your heart, you are giving the confidant one of your most valuable possessions—your time.

A grieving friend, a panic-stricken colleague, or an anxious relative who confides in you may not necessarily be eager for a solution. They are, quite often, just searching for someone to share their problems with. All they need is compassionate listening.

To handle such a situation, you may follow the three-fold path that Gaur Gopal Das, a renowned monk and motivational speaker, proposes in his second book, "Energise Your Mind."

- **Understand:** Try to first understand the problem. Understanding is often more virtuous than knowledge.

- **Feel:** To strengthen your understanding of the situation, you can try to put yourself in your friend's shoes. Every individual has unique circumstances that compound his problems; hence, any probable solution has to factor in his specific environment.
- **Act:** Take action by sharing your thoughts as guidance and not mere instructions to follow. If you can physically or emotionally help a disturbed soul, don't hesitate to extend a helping hand, but do so after you have listened to their woes with full attention.

While a judicious mind is aware of the obvious benefits of good listening skills, you may wonder how to actually enhance them.

Is there a time-tested formula? Has it been practised by generations in the past?

The art of listening holds a pivotal place in Sanatana Dharma.

Shruti, in Sanskrit, means "that which is heard" and forms the scriptural backbone of Hinduism.

Swami Chinmayananda explains that Shruti is the cumulative realisation that the sages of yesteryear were bestowed with during deep meditation. It is *apaurusheya* or not attributable to any particular individual. The state in which such divine experiences were obtained extends beyond the realms of "I" or "mine."

It is the original form of the Vedas, which were passed on from generation to generation. In fact, the Vedas are Shrutis.

Can you fathom the enormity of knowledge that only lasted in the form of words that were heard?

Such is the power of listening!

The obvious question now is how they inculcated the practice of memorising through listening.

As mentioned in the Katha Upanishad, *"He who is possessed of supreme knowledge by the concentration of mind must have his senses under control, like spirited steeds controlled by a charioteer."*

In Hindu philosophy, it is firmly believed that the Vedas and Agamas are the words of God that were given to seers through hearing.

So, for thousands of years, students learnt from their gurus by listening to them, and the Vedas remained unaltered. They could master this art by practising the verses in eleven different ways, including backwards chanting.

In priest training schools, even today, aural teaching methods are followed. The guru chants each verse once, and then the students chant it twice as a group, trying their best to match the teacher's chanting as closely as possible in terms of pronunciation and rhythm. Mastering such immaculate accuracy requires years of dedication and discipline. An early start helps; hence, some priest families send their new generations even at the age of five, when the children's memories are relatively more receptive.

Sivaya Subramuniyaswami, an American-born Hindu religious guru, says, "Because sound is the first creation, knowledge is transferred through sound of all kinds."

To master the art of listening, inculcate some of the ways that made the Vedic seers such marvellous listeners.

- **Listen to the sound of silence:** Spend some time each day listening to your inner voice. In the words of Swami Vivekananda, *"Talk to yourself once a day; otherwise, you may miss meeting an excellent person in this world."* A stronger sense of self-awareness may lead to greater empathy towards others when hearing their account.

- **Practice mindfulness:** A calm mind that is receptive to sounds (not just words) around you is also open to feeling the emotions that go into a conversation. Mindfulness also trains you to be present in the current moment, a strong attribute for a good listener. Some of the best conversations are often limited to a few words, where unspoken dialogues play a pivotal role.
- **Appreciate the value of listening:** The Vedic sages recognised the importance of listening for learning, growth, and harmony, and they worked hard to develop this ability throughout their lifetimes.

Simon Sinek, one of the most renowned modern-day motivational speakers, succinctly elucidates the art of listening: "Hearing is listening to what's said. Listening is hearing what isn't said."

So, my dear friends, listen with your heart, and you may discover nuggets of insight that may turn out to be more valuable than anything you've ever read in textbooks.

Let the light of wisdom, compassion, and bonhomie shine through the precious art of listening!

A JOYOUS JOURNEY CALLED *LIFE*

CAN YOU SMILE WHEN THE CHIPS ARE DOWN?

Discover the Key to Embracing Life's Challenges and Unleashing Inner Joy

Image by Tailor Heery (unsplash.com)

Life is an incredible roller-coaster ride full of ups and downs, joy and sadness, and a variety of experiences that help to mould us into the individuals we become. Sometimes, we may feel overwhelmed by sadness and wonder why happiness seems out of reach. Despite the challenges and difficulties, there is a hidden key that can unlock the door to eternal joy.

In this piece, we will explore the profound wisdom that His Holiness, the Dalai Lama, and Archbishop Desmond Tutu share in 'The Book of Joy'. The eight pillars of joy revealed in this must-read international bestseller uphold many of the teachings of the Buddha. By adopting these principles, we can discover how to live a happy life, regardless of the situation.

1. The Power of Perspective:

Our perspectives play a pivotal role in shaping our experiences. It is the lens through which we view the world. By choosing to see challenges as opportunities for growth and focusing on the positive aspects of our lives, we can transform even the most difficult situations into sources of joy.

> *The Dalai Lama says, "For every event in life, there are many different angles. When you look at the same event from a wider perspective, your sense of worry and anxiety reduces, and you have greater joy."*

Think about the somewhat clichéd example of a partially filled glass of water. It's entirely your perspective that will portray the image of a half-filled glass or a half-empty goblet.

A student overwhelmed by the magnitude of his syllabus may have forgotten that he is already well-versed in most of it; only the remaining parts need to be revised. When it comes to money matters, your perspective plays a critical role. We are often drawn to what we don't have rather than how much we already possess.

The Buddha teaches us through the Dhammapada that "the mind is the forerunner of all mental phenomena. All that we are is the result of what we have thought. What we think, we become." (Verse 1)

Change your perspective, and you will experience unimaginable changes in reality.

2. The Grace of Humility:

Humility is a valuable trait that cultivates appreciation and allows us to embrace the abundance of life. Recognising that we are a part of something larger than ourselves opens us up to appreciating the beauty and interconnectedness of the world. When we adopt a humble attitude, we can experience happiness not only in our own lives but also in the accomplishments and joy of those around us.

In a Tibetan prayer shared in the book, the master says, "Whenever I see someone, may I never feel superior. From the depth of my heart, may I be able to really appreciate the other person in front of me."

Such mutual respect is the cornerstone for success in several spheres of life, including the corporate environment, sports, and fostering life-long camaraderie.

Verse 50 of the Dhammapada succinctly summarises the essence of humility.

It says, "No one should criticise others or focus on the mistakes they have made. But let each person examine his or her own deeds, both good and bad."

3. The Lightness of Humour:

Laughter is a potent tool that has the ability to boost our mood and assist us in overcoming challenges. Humour has the ability to bring a feeling of lightheartedness and playfulness into our daily lives. This enables us to experience happiness and pleasure even when we are confronted with difficult situations. It urges us to avoid being overly serious and instead learn to appreciate the subtleties of life.

As Archbishop Tudu says, "When we learn to take ourselves slightly less seriously, then it is a very great help. We can see the ridiculous in us."

Modern-day life is plagued with worries about the future—the coming appraisal, the board exams, the rising expenses, and so forth. Amidst the turmoil, if you can find time to laugh wholeheartedly, you will elevate yourself to a different level where you can assess your situation from a different perspective.

The scientific community has long promoted the health benefits of laughter. As the legendary comedian Charles Chaplin said, "Laughter is the tonic, the relief, the surcease for pain."

4. The Liberating Act of Acceptance:

Acceptance is crucial to unlocking the inner peace and joy that we seek. When we accept the things that are beyond our control and welcome the course of life as it happens, we liberate ourselves from the weight of opposition. Acceptance enables us to be at peace with the current moment and value the blessings that life bestows on us.

In two simple questions, His Holiness sums up the virtue of acceptance. He asks, "Why be unhappy about something if it can be remedied? And what is the use of being unhappy if it cannot be remedied?"

The Archbishop explains that *"we are meant to live in joy. This does not mean that life will be easy or painless."* He goes on to further elucidate that the pains we experience open the door to acceptance. In so doing, it helps us face the storms of life as they pass by.

As the Buddha so famously said, "Pain is certain, suffering is optional."

Use the power of acceptance to prevent your pain points from turning into eternal suffering. Accept, adjust, and move on.

5. The Healing Power of Forgiveness:

Forgiveness is a powerful act that can transform our lives by freeing us from the negative emotions of anger, resentment, and bitterness. Choosing to forgive allows us to let go of the weight of past grievances and make room for happiness and affection to flourish in our lives. Forgiveness does not mean approving of someone's behaviour. Instead, it is an act of kindness toward ourselves that allows us to move on.

In the words of the Archbishop, "Forgiveness is the only way to heal ourselves and to be free from the past."

As Gautama said, "Remembering a wrong is like carrying a burden on the mind."

Forgiveness is not the same as forgetting. You may not forget the harm that someone has caused, but you can heal yourself with the ointment of forgiveness. In so doing, if you are able to wean yourself out of the shackles of a limiting memory, you will emerge happier.

6. The Attitude of Gratitude:

Practising gratitude is a profound way to shift our focus from what we lack to what we have in abundance in our lives. Cultivating gratitude helps us develop a profound appreciation for the small pleasures that exist in our lives. This sentiment serves as a reminder to stay in the present moment, appreciate the blessings we currently possess, and derive happiness from even the tiniest of experiences.

The Dalai Lama says the first thought in the morning, as you wake up, could be, "I am fortunate to be alive. I have a precious human life. I am not going to waste it." You are likely to have positive vibrations flowing throughout the day.

A simple yet profound message from Buddha captures the essence of gratitude: "Always be thankful for what you have; many people have nothing."

It's this sense of gratitude that opens our minds to the little joys of life. The priceless smile of your children, the blessings of the old lady selling incense sticks for survival, or the breath of fresh air on the first morning of your Himalayan escapade could all make your life an endless reservoir of happiness.

7. The Compassionate Heart:

Compassion is a fundamental aspect of our humanity. By showing kindness and empathy towards others, we have the power to spread happiness and positivity throughout the world. This ripple effect can make a significant difference in brightening up our surroundings. When we cultivate a compassionate heart, we access our natural ability to empathise and spread happiness not just to those around us, but also within ourselves.

The Buddha is believed to have said, "What is that one thing, which when you possess, you have all other virtues? It is compassion."

His Holiness, the Dalai Lama, reckons, "Too much self-centred thinking is the source of suffering. A compassionate concern for others' well-being is the source of happiness."

Giving a blanket to the homeless on a chilly winter evening is sure to warm your heart.

A teacher who is compassionate towards his slum-dwelling student is likely to extract the best out of the child and transform his life.

8. The Generosity of Spirit:

Generosity goes beyond just giving material possessions. It also includes giving our time, love, and support to others. When we share our resources and talents with others, it can bring us a deep sense of satisfaction and happiness. Selfless giving helps us fulfil our purpose and has a long-lasting impact on the people in our lives.

World religion teaches us the incredible joy of generosity. Islam calls it *Zakat*, one of the five pillars of their religious beliefs. *Tzedakah*, in Judaism, literally means "justice." The Hindu and Buddhist scriptures are replete with the morality of *Dana*, while Christianity has always upheld the nobility of charity.

When you see an older child sharing his confectionery with a less fortunate boy across the street, who may not be able to savour such delicacies, you realise the virtue of generosity.

Image from Author's own collection

Summing up:

Life is a precious gift that should be cherished, despite its many complexities. When we adopt the eight pillars of joy, which include perspective, humility, humour, acceptance, forgiveness, gratitude, compassion, and generosity, we embark on a journey towards happiness that goes beyond our current circumstances.

"The Book of Joy" teaches us that joy is not a temporary feeling but rather a state of being that we can develop within ourselves.

Let's embrace the joy that awaits us at every turn and create a life filled with profound happiness and purpose.

I leave you with the beautiful words of Mother Teresa, "Joy is a net of love by which you can catch souls."

LOVE YOURSELF, BUT HOW?

THE POWER OF SELF-COMPASSION

Eternal lessons from the Bible and the Bhagavad Gita that capture the essence of self-care.

Image by Tim Mossholder on Unsplash

In a world that glorifies achievement and success, it's natural to fall prey to self-criticism and self-doubt. We often hold ourselves to impossible standards, comparing ourselves to others and constantly striving to be better. Along the way, we lose sight of the importance of treating ourselves with the same respect and care that we show others.

This is where the teachings of the Bible and the Bhagavad Gita can help us. Both of these spiritual texts offer powerful lessons on the importance of self-compassion and the role it plays in leading a fulfilling life. Let's explore these lessons in more detail.

What does the Holy Bible say?

"Don't you know that you yourselves are God's temple and that God's Spirit dwells in your midst?"- 1 Corinthians 3:16

The Bible says that our bodies are home to the Holy Spirit. How can you then not take care of this temple that God has so lovingly created? Nourishment, rest, exercise, and, above all, self-love are the antidotes that protect this temple from untimely erosion.

Thus, in the name of the Lord God, take good care of yourself.

"Love Your Neighbour As Yourself"- Mark 12:31

This quote is often interpreted as an exhortation to love others as we love ourselves. But what if we don't love ourselves? What if we are our own worst critics, constantly putting ourselves down and setting a bar too high?

The key to understanding this quote lies in realising that the love we extend to others must begin with the love we have for ourselves. Without self-love, it is impossible to love others completely. It's also important that this love is patient, understanding, and forgiving.

Let's take a closer look at the Bhagavad Gita

"sarva-bhūta-stham ātmānaṁ

sarva-bhūtāni cātmani

īkṣate yoga-yuktātmā

sarvatra sama-darśanaḥ" -

"The Wise See The Same Self In Every Being. A self-realised Person, Sees Me Everywhere "- 6:29

The Bhagavad Gita, one of the pillars of Sanatana Dharma, carries the virtue of self-love.

The profoundness of this verse actually hinges on the simplicity of our common divine nature. We are eternally linked to that one supreme force that is the very source of our existence. Once we realise that we are sparks of the same flame, we will exude compassion and love not just for others but for ourselves as well.

The Less-Travelled Road to Self-Compassion

Here are five steps to get started:

1. Practice Mindfulness: Self-compassion begins with mindfulness—the ability to observe our thoughts and emotions without judgement. By becoming aware of our inner dialogue and the ways in which we talk to ourselves, we can start to cultivate a more compassionate and kinder relationship with ourselves.

2. Treat Yourself Like a Friend: Consider how you would respond to a close friend who was going through a tough period. How critical and severe would you be, or how supportive and encouraging? Be as generous and kind to yourself as you would be to a friend.

3. Forgive Yourself: Everyone has their share of human frailties and slip-ups. Instead of punishing yourself, learn to forgive these transgressions. Accept that you are human and that making mistakes is part of learning about yourself. Stop living in the past and start planning for the future instead—but above all, learn to enjoy the present—the 'Now' will turn into 'Then' in the blink of an eye.

4. Focus on Your Strengths: Recognise your talents and successes instead of dwelling on your flaws. Honour even the tiniest of your successes. It's always nice to get a pat on the back once in a while. You'll feel better about yourself and be able to project a more positive image of yourself if you do this.

5. Practice Self-Care: Please take care of yourself. All of your needs, physical, mental, and spiritual, must be met. Pursue recreation and relaxation. If you're feeling down, do some exercise, meditate, go for a stroll in the park, or give yourself the gift of a spa treatment, even if it feels like overindulging—after all, you're your most precious possession. When you prioritise your own needs, you'll have more compassion and kindness to give to others.

Finally, self-compassion is crucial if you want to live a life that makes a difference to others. It enables us to recognise our own pain and provide the loving care and compassion for ourselves that we so richly deserve. Both the Bible and the Bhagavad Gita teach us how to love ourselves and others unconditionally if we follow their teachings.

Keep in mind that nurturing self-compassion is a long-term goal. It takes time and effort, as well as the commitment to treat yourself kindly even while you're struggling. A compassionate self brings happiness, calm, and fulfilment, but it must be cultivated over time and with work.

The time to begin practising self-compassion is right now. Mindfulness training, self-compassion, self-forgiveness, positive self-focus, and self-care are all beneficial. You may improve your life by taking these baby steps towards a more loving and accepting connection with yourself.

As the wise teachings of the Bible and the Bhagavad Gita remind us, self-compassion is necessary not only for our personal well-being but also for those around us.

Celebrated American comedian and producer of yesteryears, Lucille Ball, once said, "Love yourself first and everything else falls into line. You really have to love yourself to get anything done in this world."

So, let us strive to love ourselves fully and extend that love to others, living in joy and peace, just as the wise have done since time immemorial.

5 LIFE-CHANGING QUOTES OF ECKHART TOLLE

AN ETERNAL JOURNEY OF SELF-DISCOVERY AND INNER TRANSFORMATION

In our fast-paced world, finding a sense of peace and fulfilment often seems elusive. Learnings from writer-philosopher Eckhart Tolle can show us the way.

Beep beep…beep beep..beep beep.. The alarm goes off. It's 6:10 a.m. as you reach out for your mobile to hit the snooze button. After two rounds of 10-minute snooze time, you force yourself to open your eyes. The instinctive first activity is to switch on the mobile data or reconnect to the WiFi. The social media alerts seem more effective than the alarm. As your left hemisphere starts activating, you get drawn to the unavoidable challenges that seem to peep mockingly from the corner of your bedroom curtains.

Sounds familiar?

It's such a common weekday morning experience for so many of us. Instead of shying away from the lurking demons of the day, can't we open the curtains and allow a bit of sunshine and fresh air to add a feeling of vitality to our mornings? Can't we take a few deep breaths and allow ourselves a smile? Be grateful that we have another day to live?

Eckhart Tolle, an internationally renowned spiritual teacher and author, offers us invaluable wisdom that can help us adopt a more optimistic perspective. In this article, we will examine five of Eckhart Tolle's most motivational statements, along with practical applications that can help you be more in the moment, strengthen your character, and handle life's inevitable ups and downs with ease.

Let's take a closer look at Eckhart Tolle's teachings on enlightenment and personal development.

"Realise deeply that the present moment is all you have. Make the NOW the primary focus of your life."

Purport: This quote emphasises the importance of living in the present moment and not being preoccupied with the past or future. It encourages individuals to fully engage with the present and find joy, peace, and fulfilment in the now.

Real-life application: In our frenzied modern-day existence, we often get caught up in worries about the future or regrets about the past. By practising mindfulness and focusing on the present, we can become more aware of the beauty and opportunities around us. Embracing the present moment allows us to make the most of every experience and find gratitude in the simple things.

The most joyous moment for me every day is seeing my son's smiling face in the morning. It's such a simple thing, but it refreshes my mind more than anything else. It's a moment I revisit in my mind often throughout the day, as it acts as the biggest motivator to go through the challenges of mundane life.

Do I wish to trade that for material glories that keep me away from the magic moment?

The answer is an emphatic NO.

However, does it push me toward steeper goals in life?

It sure as hell does!

We often find our biggest motivation in commonplace things happening around us. You just need to still your mind to observe those precious moments and then unleash the power within.

"Life isn't as serious as the mind makes it out to be."

Purport: This is a great reminder that our thoughts and interpretations often create unnecessary drama and seriousness in our lives. By recognising the transient nature of life's challenges, we can cultivate a lighter and more joyful perspective.

Real-life application: When faced with difficulties or setbacks, it's easy to get caught up in negative thinking and amplify the seriousness of the situation. However, by consciously choosing to detach from excessive worry or overthinking, we can approach challenges with a more positive mindset. Have you tried Jay Shetty's 'fist exercise'? It's a simple practice: whenever you feel overwhelmed with seemingly insurmountable challenges, just take a deep breath and curl your fingers into a fist; as you breathe out, uncurl the fingers. Do this exercise for just 2-3 minutes and experience the immediate calmness that ensues, decluttering your mind.

This shift in perspective allows us to find creative solutions and maintain inner peace.

> As the great Charles Chaplin famously said, "A day without laughter is a day wasted." Allow the kid inside you to peek out once or twice a day. A giggle, a smile, or a hearty laugh can go a long way toward healing your wounds.

Choose to avoid that horrifying murder mystery on Netflix before going to bed; instead, play a light comedy that titillates your senses. Burst out into an unabashed guffaw that washes away your worries, albeit momentarily.

When you return to those serious thoughts, your mind will be at ease to seek solutions to the problems rather than fret over them.

"The power is in you. The answer is in you. And you are the answer to all your searches."

Purport: This quote highlights the inherent power and wisdom within each individual. It encourages self-reliance and self-empowerment, reminding us that we have the capacity to find answers and create positive change within ourselves.

Real-life application: In times of uncertainty or when facing important decisions, we often seek external validation or look for answers outside ourselves. However, by turning inward and trusting our intuition, we can tap into our own inner guidance. Embracing self-reflection and self-trust empowers us to make choices aligned with our values and aspirations.

The Holy Bible likens our bodies to the abode of the Holy Spirit (1 Corinthians 6:19). In several verses of the Bhagavad Gita, we are reminded that every living entity is a spirit soul, part and parcel of the Absolute Supreme.

Thus, we hold the power to shape our lives like no one else does. Believe in yourselves and in the eternal blessings of the Lord, and march towards your goals with conviction.

"Accept—then act. Whatever the present moment contains, accept it as if you had chosen it. Always work with it, not against it."

Purport: This quote emphasises the importance of accepting the present moment, regardless of its circumstances. By embracing what is, we can move forward with clarity and effectiveness instead of resisting or dwelling on what we cannot change.

Real-life application: Life often presents us with situations beyond our control, such as a job loss or the untimely demise of a loved one. By accepting these circumstances and reframing them as opportunities for growth, we can shift our mindset and take proactive steps towards positive change. Acceptance enables us to channel our energy into finding solutions and making the best of any situation.

A delicate slice of my life to emphasise the point.

With dreams of a glorified life abroad with my family, I quit my job in late 2019. Cut to March 2020, the world came to a standstill in light of one of the scariest pandemics in recent times. Instead of pressing the panic button, I took a pause to assess the situation. The journey of restarting my life began by accepting the unchangeable global condition. In the bargain, I have discovered my Ikigai and am pursuing my life's goals as a writer with renewed vigour.

Accept, assess, and ascend to greater heights.

"Worry pretends to be necessary but serves no useful purpose."

Purport: This one is a masterpiece in emphasising that worrying about the future or dwelling on past events does not contribute positively to our lives. It highlights that worrying is often a futile activity that drains our energy and distracts us from the present moment.

Real-life application: In our daily lives, we often find ourselves consumed by worry and anxiety. We may fret about things that are beyond our control or replay past mistakes in our minds. However, this quote reminds us that worrying serves no productive purpose and only adds unnecessary stress to our lives. By letting go of worry and focusing on the present, we can channel our energy into actions that are within our control, leading to a more positive and fulfilling life.

The effervescent monk Gaur Gopal Das has given a delightful analogy to the above purport in his first book, 'Life's Amazing Secrets'. He reckons that when we face a problem in our lives, we should adopt a two-fold approach. The first question to ask ourselves is, "Can this problem be solved?" If the answer is yes, then we should divert our attention to the probable solution. If, on the other hand, the answer is no, then is there any merit in worrying about it? We should rather let time be the natural healer.

In a world filled with distractions and pressures, Eckhart Tolle's teachings provide a guiding light towards inner peace and a positive mindset. By embracing the power of now and trusting our inner wisdom, we can transform our lives and experience a profound sense of fulfilment. Let us remember Tolle's timeless quotes and apply their wisdom in our daily lives, knowing that the journey to a more positive outlook begins within ourselves.

So, take a deep breath, let go of the past and future, and embrace the beauty of the present moment—for it holds the key to a truly enriched and joyful life.

SACHIN, THE MODERN-DAY ARJUNA

WHAT CHAMPIONS ARE MADE OF!

"Saaacchiin Saaachiin…." For any cricket lover across the globe, this was a familiar chant that reverberated across stadiums in the 1990s and 2000s every time the maestro entered the cricketing arena with the bat in hand.

So many accolades have been showered on the living legend that there's nothing new to write about.

However, having followed the icon so closely throughout his illustrious career, I find an uncanny familiarity with some of the characteristics of Arjuna, the warrior prince from the epic Mahabharata.

Is Sachin the true modern-day Arjuna?

The 1994 Arjuna Award recipient has been the epitome of discipline, dedication, and determination—some of the critical aspects of character-building that Arjuna showed us.

Arjuna is recognised as an archer par excellence. The Mahabharata is replete with tales of his mastery of the bow and arrow. From piercing the lone bird on a tree to nailing a rotating fish by just looking at its reflection to finally playing the pivotal role in the Kurukshetra, Arjuna demonstrated his god-gifted talent at every opportunity.

Similarly, page after page can be filled with instances of Sachin's extraordinary wizardry with the willow.

However, there were other characters in the Mahabharata, like Ekalavya and Karna, who could rival Arjuna with their sheer talent. Much like Vinod Kambli or even the great Brian Lara, who were compared with Sachin at certain stages of his career.

But what sets a genius apart from other greats?

Let's take a closer look at the four key virtues displayed by Arjuna that manifested through this legendary sportsman. Some of the qualities that separate the greatest from the greats are:

1. Devotion: Arjuna was deeply devoted to Lord Krishna and followed his guidance without question. The backdrop of one of the pillars of Sanatana Dharma, the Bhagavad Gita, is his devotion to Lord Krishna. When Arjuna hesitated to fight in the Kurukshetra war due to the presence of his relatives and loved ones on the opposing side, Krishna imparted divine knowledge to him, and Arjuna humbly accepted it, dedicating himself wholeheartedly to his duty.

His devotion was not just to the divine; his unflinching dedication to his trade was also exemplary. Thus, he became the favourite student of his guru, Dronacharya.

Resemblance with Sachin: Well, the immense contribution of coach extraordinaire Ramakant Achrekar in the making of the legend is now a matter of folklore. Sachin's devotion to his art was evident even at the tender age of 10 or 11 when he started practising regularly with Achrekar Sir. Riding pillion on his scooter, travelling from one ground to the other, showed his tremendous dedication to the game of cricket.

When dedication transforms into devotion, it sets you on your way to greatness, irrespective of the vocation you choose.

2. Courage: On numerous occasions, but especially in the heat of combat, Arjuna showed exceptional bravery. One particularly noteworthy illustration of this may be seen in the Virata Parva, in which Arjuna, cloaked in the identity of a eunuch dancing teacher named Brihannala, engaged in a heroic battle against Kaurava troops in order to defend the kingdom of Matsya.

Resemblance with Sachin: It's hard to pick one or two such moments from Sachin's great career where he displayed praiseworthy courage against daunting bowling attacks. However, two incidents that stand out for me both came in his maiden Test series against arch-rivals Pakistan on their home turf.

On the last test match of the series at Sialkot, the 16-year-old Sachin got hit on the nose by a Waqar Younis riser. Without paying any heed to the bloody nose, the youngster stood up against the fearsome pace attack comprising some of the contemporary greats, like Wasim Akram, Imran Khan, and a lethal Waqar Younis. The flick of his pads and the backfoot punch through the covers, immediately after being hit, spoke volumes about his resilience and willingness to compete against the very best.

The other instance came in an exhibition one-day match on the same 1989 tour of Pakistan. Sachin tore into one of the greatest leg-spinners of all time, Abdul Qadir, smashing him for four sixes in one over.

When you say goodbye to your inner inhibitions, you open the door for everlasting success.

3. Perseverance: Arjuna faced many trials and tribulations during his thirteen years of exile, yet he never lost focus on his preparation for the war against the Kauravas. He searched for divine weapons and studied advanced combat strategies in order to arm himself appropriately for the impending war against the Kauravas.

Resemblance with Sachin: A 22-year-long tenure at the highest level would test anyone's persistence. Tendulkar fought his way through rough patches and resultant criticism, team failures for which responsibilities were often thrust upon his shoulders, and career-threatening injuries.

His knock against the formidable Pakistan attack, led by Wasim Akram at Chennai in 1998, is testimony to his perseverance amidst excruciating pain from back spasms. It was his first major injury after nearly a decade of international cricket.

If this was not enough, he had to endure a severely distressing experience during the 2004-05 season with tennis elbow. A painful condition that many would have considered a time to call for the curtains. But his passion for the game meant a strong comeback after more than a year's suffering.

In the words of Sachin's great friend and rival, the late Shane Warne, "Never give up. Just absolutely never give up."

4. Humility: Arjuna was respectful and modest despite his extraordinary abilities and family history. In the Vana Parva, Arjuna exhibited his humility by paying respect to numerous sages and listening closely to their lessons.

Resemblance with Sachin: From his days as the first overseas cricketer for Yorkshire until his last test innings against the West Indies, Sachin remained an ardent student of the game. He would scrutinise each and every inning with his brother Ajit and try to figure out areas for improvement.

Such humbleness in the face of heightened glory kept him at the top of his game until he called it a day. People who have known him closely highlight this side of the man in the book "Sachin@50- Celebrating a Maestro," conceptualised and curated by cricket connoisseur Boria Majumdar.

These character traits of Arjuna serve as valuable lessons for all of us, demonstrating the importance of courage, devotion, perseverance, and humility in our own lives. Sachin is one of the greatest manifestations of these virtues, which are the founding pillars of success in every walk of life.

Everyone may not be as gifted as Arjuna or Sachin Tendulkar, but by inculcating strong work ethics and a value system, you can be the best version of yourself.

EASTER – A TIME FOR INNER RESURRECTION

MOVING BEYOND RELIGIOUS SIGNIFICANCE

From Resurrection to Redemption: Exploring the Deeper Meaning of Easter

Photo by Geralt (Pixabay.com)

Easter is a time of year that holds great significance for many people around the world. It is a time when we celebrate life, renewal, and hope. For Christians, it is a time to reflect on the resurrection of Jesus Christ and the promise of redemption that it represents. But beyond the symbolism of the Easter egg and the significance of the cross, there is a rich history and tradition behind this holiday. So, whether you're a believer or simply curious about the history of Easter, join us as we journey from resurrection to redemption and discover the true meaning of this ancient observance.

The history behind Easter

The origins of Easter can be traced back to ancient times, long before the birth of Christianity. It was a time when people celebrated the arrival of spring and the renewal of life after the long, dark winter. It was frequently characterised by feasting, dancing, and other celebrations in many cultures.

For instance, the Anglo-Saxons called it Eostre, after their goddess of fertility and spring, a theory propounded by the eighth-century English monk Bede. In most European nations, the festival stems from the Jewish tradition of Passover. In Greek, it's Pascha; in Italian, it's Pasqua; the Danes celebrate it as Paaske, while the French call it Paques. The Germans named the festival Ostern after the goddess Ostara.

Despite its pagan roots, Easter became an important Christian observance, commemorating the resurrection of Jesus Christ. It was first celebrated in the 2nd century, and over time, it became one of the most important events in the Christian calendar.

The Council of Nicaea in 325 decreed that the first Sunday following the full moon after the spring equinox would be observed as Easter. Thus, according to the Gregorian calendar, Easter falls on a Sunday between March 22 and April 25.

Cross, Resurrection, and Redemption—cornerstones of Easter

The resurrection of Jesus Christ is one of the most important doctrines in Christianity. It is regarded as a supernatural occurrence that demonstrates the might of God and the assurance of eternal life. It shows the sanctity of the scriptural messages and marks the beginning of the Kingdom of God.

The cross is a sign of hope for a fresh beginning, in addition to being a symbol of the suffering and sacrifice that it represents. In essence, what does it symbolise? It shows that challenges are part and parcel of our lives. But with faith in God, we can overcome every hurdle and emerge victorious. It also denotes that the beloved Son of God has taken on our behalf the ultimate penalty for our sins. Thus, we leave the past behind and bask in the glory of a renewed life.

Easter is centred on the concept of redemption. Merriam-Webster defines the word "redeem" in several ways. Among them, the most contextual meanings are:

- to free from what distresses or harms: such as to free from captivity by payment of ransom
- to extricate from or help to overcome something detrimental
- to release from blame or debt
- to be free from the consequences of sin

The dictionary further adds that to redeem is to reform, 'to change for the better.'

The concept of redemption inspires us to look beyond our faults and shortcomings. It teaches us to cast our minds on the positive qualities of ourselves as well as the people around us.

"The kingdom of God cometh not with observation: neither shall they say, Lo here! or, lo there! for, behold, the kingdom of God is within you" (Luke 17:20-21).

The Various Easter Customs and What They Signify

Image by: Silviarita (Pixabay.com)

Easter traditions are steeped in symbolic items that have profound religious connotations. The Easter egg is a symbol of new life that is associated with the idea of rebirth. The Easter bunny represents fertility and abundance.

The beautiful Easter lilies adorn the churches and homes of Christians around the globe. The blossoming of the fresh flowers is a mark of purity and rebirth, or a fresh beginning.

The gifting of Easter baskets carries the blessings of a new life and the promise of renewal.

Easter Is Eternal—Rejuvenate, Refresh, Restart

As we travel from the event of the resurrection to the event of our redemption, we are reminded of the significance of love, hope, and trust. Easter is a time when we should examine our own lives and think about the ways in which we can refresh both ourselves and the connections we have with others.

It is time to forgive oneself for prior transgressions and look forward to the opportunities presented by fresh starts. It is a time to remember that even in the darkest of times, there is always a chance for renewal and rebirth, and it is a time to remember to look beyond ourselves and to concentrate on the good in others.

"Therefore, as God's chosen people, holy and dearly loved, clothe yourselves with compassion, kindness, humility, gentleness, and patience. Bear with each other and forgive one another if any of you has a grievance against someone. Forgive as the Lord forgave you." (Colossians 3:12-13)

Easter allows us to contemplate this message from the Lord. Think about ways in which you can incorporate its teachings into your own life, regardless of the religious tradition to which you adhere. It's time to realise the virtues of gratitude, forgiveness, and compassion as the cornerstones of humanity.

In the end, Easter is a celebration of life, renewal, and optimism; it also serves as a reminder that there is always a chance for redemption and renewal, regardless of where we are on our journey.

So, my friends, the best tribute to the unparalleled sacrifice that Jesus made for us is to leave behind our past trauma, break the barriers of negative thoughts, and embrace a new life in the name of our beloved Lord.

Reference:

1. https://www.britannica.com/event/First-Council-of-Nicaea-325

THIS TOO SHALL PASS

5 KEY LESSONS WE LEARN DURING TROUBLED TIMES

Whether it was King Solomon or Abraham Lincoln who popularised this phrase, the powerful message is undeniable!

Image by National Cancer Institute (Unsplash.com)

We have all had our share of ups and downs in life. Be it from genuine well-wishers or just uninterested observers, we have also received somewhat cliched motivational statements like the title of this piece or "every cloud has a silver lining," "there's light at the end of the tunnel," and so forth.

Have you ever wondered whether these are just comforting words? Or old adages to make you feel less miserable? Or is there a deeper message hidden somewhere in these overused one-liners?

I believe they do divert our attention to the impermanence of the circumstances that threaten to choke us. But at a deeper level, they also bring out the immense learning potential that lies within those very occurrences.

So when the chips are down, what are those critical lessons that can propel you to greater heights in life?

Image by Kyle Glenn (Unsplash.com)

Before we answer the intriguing question above, let's look at some of the problems that people face today. Though this may seem to be generalising to some extent, these are the pressing circumstances that push us to the verge of collapse.

- **Financial crisis:** Financial worries are a major cause of several mental afflictions like depression, stress, substance abuse, impulsive behaviour, sleep disorders and so forth. It also has a direct bearing on your physical well-being as you try to cut corners to make ends meet, resulting in poor nutrition, lack of necessary healthcare, etc.
- **Emotional setback:** A loss of a loved one, break-ups or separations, relocation leading to detachment from your friend circle, or any other mental trauma can set you back in life.
- **Health problems:** A serious accident leading to loss of limbs or prolonged treatment for an ailment can seem like a never-ending battle.
- **A new venture or a series of new endeavours going wrong:** Even if it doesn't lead to a major monetary loss, it can affect your self-esteem. Overcoming such stumbling blocks could seem impossible.

These apparent roadblocks are ideal times for introspection. You may discover some life-altering lessons during these phases. Some of my personal discoveries are:

Finding your calling: Difficult times often open doors that you never knew existed. A loss of employment may give you the opportunity to explore your latent talents. Lo and behold, you could well discover the vocation that transforms your life into something you may occasionally have just dreamt of. In Japan, they call it Ikigai, a concept that is one of the secrets of their long lives and everlasting happiness.

Similarly, a failed relationship may invite your soulmate into your life. You may well be experiencing true love and blissful bonding for the first time in your life.

A broken leg that keeps you bedridden for six months could actually produce the bestseller that you always wanted to write but couldn't devote your time and attention to.

Fortifying your self-belief: Turbulent times are meant to make you stronger mentally and emotionally. As the former Prime Minister of the United Kingdom, John Major, famously said, "When your back is against the wall, there is only one thing to do, turn around and fight."

Tough times make you look within to seek refuge. You may discover that you are stronger than you believed and have the resolve to fight back.

This is also a time to remove the rust from your skills. Great sports personalities often use their bad phases to work on their technical glitches and come back stronger.

The great Michael Jordan said, "I've missed more than 9,000 shots in my career. I've lost almost 300 games. Twenty-six times, I've been trusted to take the game-winning shot and missed. I've failed over and over and over again in my life. And that is why I succeed."

Change in your money mindset: This is applicable to circumstances that have a bearing on your wealth. One mode is to press the panic button, but the other alternative is to radically change your perception of money. When you realise that everything that's happening is temporary, you also start believing that the depletion of wealth is also momentary.

This thought process alone can turn you into a money magnet. However, what it will do for sure is increase your appetite for risk. With nothing more to lose, you can afford to be more aggressive than you normally would. Yes, it doesn't necessitate outrageously irrational decisions, but it will help you break the shackles of resistance (read the piece, 'Resist Resistance, if you haven't already. If you have, you might want to re-read it).

Gratitude: Difficult times teach you to be humble. You also tend to become more compassionate toward others as you realise that there are several co-passengers on the boat you are sailing in.

As Gautama Buddha said, "Let us rise up and be thankful, for if we didn't learn a lot, at least we learnt a little, and if we didn't learn a little, at least we didn't get sick, and if we got sick, at least we didn't die; so, let us all be thankful."

After the initial phase where everything feels like a whirlwind, you attain a degree of calmness that makes way for gratitude. You may have lost something (or someone) really dear, but what you still have is precious.

I learnt to practice gratitude consciously by thanking the Lord for everything that He has bestowed on me: food, shelter, friends, and above all, a loving family.

Spiritual awakening: Everything I've said so far comes from a stronger faith in the Absolute Supreme.

Meditation, mindfulness practices, empathy, and gratitude all culminate in reinforcing your faith in the Lord. As you ponder over your predicament, you hear his words, "fear not, I am with you, be not dismayed, for I am your God, I will strengthen you, I will help you, I will uphold you with my righteous right hand."
(Isaiah 41:10)

With this assurance from the Lord to be our eternal guiding star, what adversities can hold you back?

Utilise this passing period to discover yourself, spend time with your family, hone your skills, and emerge as a more formidable force.

The famous dialogue of Sylvester Stallone from the Rocky Balboa series rings in my ears, "It ain't about how hard you hit. It's about how hard you can get hit and keep moving forward. How much you can take and keep moving forward. That's how winning is done!"

ARE THE EIGHTFOLD PATHS OF BUDDHISM PASSÉ?

A WALK IN TRUTH: EIGHT STEPS TO A RIGHTEOUS LIFE

Awaken your inner Buddha through the enlightened words of the Gautama.

Image by Mattia Faloretti (Unsplash.com)

The Sanskrit word 'Budh' means 'to awaken,' and its past participle, 'Buddha,' denotes the 'awakened or enlightened one'.

The spiritual journey of Gautama (Sanskrit) or Gotama (Pali) from the riches of his kingdom to the bodhi tree of eternal light at Bodh Gaya in India is a life lesson in itself.

In this discourse, we will look at the famous Eightfold Path of Buddhism and seek its relevance in today's world. They are the crux of the Fourth Truth that Gautama discovered en route to his spiritual quest and are highly regarded in the Buddhist fraternity.

So what are these Eightfold Paths (Sanskrit: Astangika Marga; Pali: Atthangika-magga)?

Right Understanding:

Buddhism teaches us that the ceaseless pursuit of our material yearnings results in grief. What's more, once we satisfy our wishes, they grow more prominent, creating an infinite loop of unhappiness. By gaining clarity on the truth of our existence, we are able to free ourselves from the endless loop of enduring pain and difficulty.

Present-day perspective: In an age of increasing materialism, it may be asking a bit too much to forgo all material desires. However, can we stop being obsessed with our material pursuits? An adventure camp with your family could be more blissful than a lonely vacation in an exotic location. It helps to take a pause every now and then to prioritise our wants and categorise them into:

a) must-haves: the basics—food, shelter, clothes, essential medical care, primary education, etc.

b) desirables: the good-to-haves—a safe and comfortable car, an advanced home security system, higher education, occasional dine-outs, and so forth.

c) dispensables: the extravagant—business class travel when economy class serves the purpose, designer clothes and jewellery, high-end (and often purposeless) gadgets, and the list goes on.

Surely, the list varies from person to person, the message is loud and clear—prioritise.

Right Thought:

Buddha taught us that our thoughts are incredibly influential and can shape how we feel and act. Realising this teaches us to keep our intentions good in order to create positive outcomes.

Present-day perspective: The corporate rate race has instilled a desire to stay ahead of our peers. While healthy competition has its merits, our intentions should guide us toward holistic growth rather than personal gains at the expense of others. Focusing on personal development has more long-term virtues than trying to demean your colleagues and associates.

Right Speech:

According to Buddha, words hold immense power, and the ideas they represent can have lasting impacts. He shared four pieces of advice to help us use our words responsibly: Be honest, don't indulge in rumour-mongering, avoid saying anything that may harm others and abstain from mindless chatter. It's always important to practise being honest and respectful when interacting with others. Being mindful of your words and only speaking when appropriate can lead to productive conversations that can positively impact your relationships.

Present-day perspective: The power of words, whether they are written or spoken, can have a profound effect on our relationships. A hasty text message or verbal abuse can, in a matter of moments, undo the efforts put into building a bond among partners, friends, and coworkers.

However, it is often our thoughts that trigger such outbursts, so if we can monitor our thoughts, we can avoid disasters. Try whispering the sentence in your mind before speaking it out; it may help quieten an agitated mind. Read and re-read before clicking on the send button; editing or replacing a few words, adding an emoji, etc., can drastically change the impact of a written message.

Right Action:

We can demonstrate our understanding of Dhamma (truth or law) through the way we conduct ourselves. Our thoughts and actions are interrelated and together have a significant impact on our character and development. Buddha teaches us to live with integrity, following the three basic principles:

A) Do not harm others

B) Do not be dishonest

C) Stay away from sexual misconduct

Furthermore, we should also strive to help ensure that others can live with similar moral values.

Present-day perspective: It's all a vicious cycle that starts with our minds. Amidst the cacophony of noise that our thoughts make, it's nearly impossible to pick out the best ones every single time. Satan may tempt you with thoughts like, "There's no harm in taking a small bribe as long as you don't make it a habit." If you give in to such provocation once, you may find it irresistible the next time a similar opportunity comes along. Be righteous in your actions, and soon the thoughts will start to align themselves.

Right Livelihood:

According to Buddha, one should always try to make a living through lawful and peaceful means. This includes abstaining from professions that involve:

1) weaponry

2) misuse of human and animal life

3) slaughtering and butchering

4) intoxicating substances (e.g., drugs and alcohol).

Present-day perspective: Well, this could be a point of debate if we think of imbibing them in totality. Nevertheless, the essence is actionable if modified for our modern context. For example:

- You can choose not to hunt and eat animals unless you need to in order to stay alive. Instead, non-vegetarians can eat meat from animals that were raised to be eaten.
- While slavery is almost extinct, we can use compassion and empathy in dealing with our subordinates.
- Use weapons of mass destruction only for protection and not for acts of terrorism.
- Utilise drugs for making life-saving medicines rather than substances of abuse.

Right Effort:

The teachings of Buddha encourage us to make a conscious effort towards pure thoughts and actions. Whilst striving for this, we can eventually lead ourselves to a state of well-being and peace. The Buddha preached the importance of putting various levels of effort into different kinds of practices, with greater input required for spiritual growth than for minor ones. Higher levels will require more dedication and hard work, but it is worth all the effort.

1. Taking proactive steps to prevent negative thoughts is the first step in the process.
2. The level after that might be getting rid of a bad thought or feeling.
3. Following that, you should strive to think positively and cultivate warm sentiments.
4. Pushing yourself to the highest level will require dedication, effort, and willpower. Doing so can help you cultivate a strong and harmonious state of mind, allowing you to reach your goals more effectively.

Present-day perspective: Countering recurring negative thoughts and overcoming habitual bad actions takes tenacity. Every time your boss screams at you, you may feel, "Here he goes again." But he could be the same person who defends his team in front of the top management like a rock of Gibraltar. Would you prefer a sweet-talking backstabber who passes the buck whenever he is cornered by his superiors? Maybe by recognising the good qualities in your boss, you may, over time, influence him to calm down and address his team in a more relaxed manner. An exercise like this is surely long-drawn-out, but is worth every bit of the effort.

Right Mindfulness:

One of the most powerful teachings of Buddhism is mindfulness. This practice has even made its way into modern psychotherapeutic practices. Mindfulness is about living in the now with an attitude of non-judgemental acceptance and appreciation. Gautam Buddha also referred to the four foundations on which mindfulness is built—contemplation of the body, feelings, states of mind, and phenomena (environment).

By practising mindfulness, we can become more aware of our thoughts, actions, and feelings and less affected by our cravings, which often take over our minds. This can help us break free from regrets from the past or worries about the future.

Present-day perspective: Have you ever been so stressed out by your list of things to do that you almost froze for a few minutes without doing anything? With so many things happening around us, the mind is a maze of thoughts and feelings.

The significance of mindfulness is even more profound today than ever before. When we pay less attention to how our bodies and minds feel, we are often better able to do the tasks at hand.

Right Concentration:

Right concentration is the key to transforming your mind and building mental discipline. It's an important exercise in Buddhist thought and practice and forms the cornerstone of meditation.

Buddha spoke of four stages of meditation, called Dhyana, which can help you reach deeper levels of concentration and awareness.

1. In the initial phase of focus, all thoughts and feelings which act as mental blocks are removed, and a sense of joy is experienced. It is then that one can reach their highest potential.
2. Once you reach the next stage, your mind is at peace, and you experience true bliss.
3. As we enter the third stage of our journey, serenity and joy start to slowly dwindle away.
4. At the last stage, all feelings of bliss are replaced by the stillness of the mind—an even deeper kind of contentment. This is what Buddha referred to as true joy.

Present-day perspective: From stress and anxiety management to improved concentration and sharper memory, the impact of meditation on our mental well-being can hardly be overemphasised. Modern scientific research shows that it may help with pain relief, lowering blood pressure, getting a good night's sleep, and a number of other things we do every day.

Irrespective of your religious beliefs, the tenets of Buddhism have a lot to offer to help navigate the hurdles of modern life. Finding the "Buddha" in us could be a lifelong mission, but following the teachings of Gautama can help us get there.

I leave you with the profound thought of the great Greek philosopher Socrates: "All men's souls are immortal, but the souls of the righteous are immortal and divine."

SOME SPINE-CHILLING WORDS OF THE SWAMI

COMPELLING QUOTES OF THE 'CYCLONIC MONK FROM INDIA'

These power-statements are certain to shake you out of inaction and propel you on your onwards journey!

Image by Sketchepedia on Freepik

From Naren to Vivekananda

Swami Vivekananda is hailed as one of the greatest spiritual leaders of India, and his teachings continue to inspire millions around the world. However, behind his towering persona lay the formative years that were marked by a deep sense of confusion and uncertainty. The crossover from Naren to Vivekananda is a remarkable one, fuelled by an unwavering commitment to self-discovery and spiritual growth.

Born Narendranath Datta, he grew up in a household steeped in religious and cultural traditions. Nevertheless, it was his encounter with Sri Ramakrishna Paramahamsa that proved to be the turning point in his life.

Under the guidance of his mystic spiritual guru, Naren underwent a profound transformation. He shed his doubts and fears and embraced a life of selflessness and service. He also gained a deep understanding of the essence of Vedanta and other spiritual teachings. Narendranath emerged from this life-altering experience as Swami Vivekananda, a beacon of hope and inspiration for generations.

Swamiji's teachings remind us of the importance of embracing our true selves and living a life of purpose and meaning.

Among his several thought-provoking quotes, I have picked three of my favourites to share with you.

> *"Arise, awake, and stop not till the goal is reached."*

Originally found in the Katha Upanishad, this slightly modified version is one of Swami Vivekananda's most powerful quotes.

Context: Swami Vivekananda visited the famine-hit township of Ramnad on January 29, 1897. A mass of starving commoners with shabby clothes, dishevelled hair, and dreary eyes received a revitalising dose of Swamiji's soul-stirring speech. His opening lines were, "Let us all work hard, my brethren; this is no time for sleep. On our work depends the coming of the India of the future. She is only sleeping. Arise, and awake, and see her seated here, on the eternal throne, rejuvenated and more glorious than she ever was—this Motherland of ours."

A few days later, in Kumbakonam, in another mass announcement, he added, "Stop not till the goal is reached."

The quote became famous all over the world, and it is still one of Swami Vivekananda's strongest messages.

Mahatma Gandhi and Subhas Chandra Bose, the spearheads of India's freedom movement, were deeply influenced by Swami Vivekananda.

Even without engaging in political warfare with British colonialism, the saffron-robed monk on a mission had a big impact on the whole country with his powerful words. The youth icon ignited the minds of several patriots and left an indelible imprint on India's freedom struggle.

The purport of the quote: In a deeper context, this famous line draws our attention to the state of perpetual slumber that some of us have fallen into. While our senses are attuned to the outside world, our inner selves are yet to be awakened. The statement attempts to stir us out of this stupor and compel us to take a deep dive within ourselves. Only when we are aligned with our true selves can we set goals that become the very purpose of our existence. Once we attain that state, we should pull through all hurdles and hindrances to achieve the goals that we have set our minds upon.

"All the powers in the universe are already ours. It is we who have put our hands before our eyes and cry that it is dark. Know that there is no darkness around us."

Context: Swami Vivekananda said this in a lecture on "Practical Vedanta" on November 10, 1896, in London.

Swamiji explained that Vedanta teaches oneness, one life throughout, and that faith covers all of life. From forest caves to busy streets and cities, we must apply theories and comprehend how they work. Many of these thoughts have come from monarchs, who are supposed to lead the busiest lives. The Bhagavad-Gita illustrates the practical Vedanta theory of intense action but eternal calmness. This is Vedanta's secret to success, and without it, the walls surrounding us would be inert.

The purport of the quote: Vedanta tells us that we have all the capabilities within us to shape our lives the way we want. Such prowess has always been with us. It's our self-imposed limitations that have created a veil of non-existent darkness. We should come out of this cocoon and embrace the immense potential that lies within. Weakness and impurity are products of an ignorant mind; Vedanta considers such thoughts as fools' cries.

He further adds, "Everything is ours already—infinite purity, freedom, love, and power."

Thus, my friends, shed your inhibitions and march ahead with the conviction that you possess all that you need to succeed.

"Take up one idea. Make that one idea your life — think of it, dream of it, live on that idea. Let the brain, muscles, nerves, every part of your body, be full of that idea, and just leave every other idea alone. This is the way to success.."

Context: Swami Vivekananda shared this philosophy in the book "Raja Yoga" (Chapter VI- Pratyahara and Dharana).

Swami explains in this chapter that the amalgamation of internal organs, external stimulants, and the mind results in perception. A mind under control would not yield to perceptions. While *Pratyahara* is the art of mind control and is achieved through years of sustained effort, Dharana trains us to focus on one body part at a time.

The chapter goes deeper into an ideal life for yogis, with recommended diets and the benefits of yoga. However, the crux of the message in this chapter is to gain complete control of our minds and not allow others to influence them. And the way to do it is to focus on one goal at a time.

The purport of the quote: Among several common threads of successful personalities across the world, the foremost is an obsessive focus on their goals. That's what separates the great from the good, the achievers from the dreamers. Swami Vivekananda draws our attention to this 'Yogic' discipline of the mind. Unwavering focus and unrelenting hunger to attain our goals are the 'super-formula' for success. To achieve this, we must control the fluttering mind.

He further adds, "To succeed, you must have tremendous perseverance, tremendous will."

The study of Swami Vivekananda's philosophies and ideals could be a lifelong journey. The light of wisdom shines at every stage of this enlightening odyssey.

In the words of Nobel Prize-winning French novelist Romain Rolland, "The thought of this warrior prophet of India left a deep mark upon the United States . . . . I cannot touch these sayings of his... without giving a thrill through my body like an electric shock. And what shocks, what transports must have been produced when in burning words they issued from the lips of the hero!"

References:

1. https://indiachapter.in/index.php?/user/article/2/33/39
2. https://www.swamivivekananda.guru/2017/06/29/practical-vedanta-part-i-delivered-in-london-10th-november-1896/
3. https://www.swamivivekananda.guru/2017/07/24/chapter-vi-pratyahara-and-dharana/
4. https://ramakrishna.org/vivekanandatribute.html

WHAT IF YOU CAN'T 'LET GO'?

BREAKING THE CLICHE OF THE SELF-HELP REALM

Letting go is tough; what else can you do?

Image by Paul Pastourmatzis (Unsplash)

When it comes to mind management, one of the most common pieces of advice we receive from spiritual gurus and proponents of the "power of the mind" is to let go of the demons of our past. These memories have the potential to wreak havoc with our mental equilibrium. They can range from childhood abuses (both physical and mental) to more recent familial disharmony caused by the lockdown.

Irrespective of their recency or severity, negative memories of the past can act as barriers to progress. If we are constantly bogged down by something that has gone wrong in the past, then how do we concentrate on the present and build our future?

Aside from psychiatric treatment, which may be needed depending on the situation, there are a lot of non-medical ways to deal with trauma from the past. We may discuss some of those in another discourse.

However, the pressing question that keeps cropping up in my mind is: do these focused efforts to eradicate traumatic memories bring those very thoughts back to our minds with greater intensity?

What if we could train the turbulent mind to just accept the scars and let them be?

The warrior prince Arjuna's conversation with Lord Krishna at Kurukshetra forms one of the pillars of Hinduism. The Bhagavad Gita, in the words of Aldous Huxley, "...is one of the most clear and comprehensive summaries of perennial philosophy ever revealed; hence its enduring value is subject not only to India but to all of humanity."

Here we find the great archer surrendering to the indomitable power of the mind and saying, "The mind is very restless, turbulent, strong, and obstinate, O Krishna. It appears to me that it is more difficult to control than the wind." (BG:6.34)

Lord Krishna, admitting the potency of the mind, thus responds "…..O mighty-armed son of Kunti, what you say is correct; the mind is indeed very difficult to restrain. But by practice and detachment, it can be controlled." (BG:6.35)

The two most destructive weapons at the disposal of our minds are guilt and grudges. Let us explore how we can control these overwhelming emotions.

Guiding past guilt

Guilt can be of two types, as Gaur Gopal Das, one of the most popular monks from India and a widely followed spiritual speaker, mentions in his book, "Energise Your Mind." Reasonable guilt stems from a mistake that we have made in the past, either deliberately or inadvertently, that has caused harm to someone—in most cases, a known person.

Unreasonable guilt usually arises in more complex circumstances. Suppose three college friends, Tom, Dick, and Harry, end up in the same department in an organization. They have all worked hard throughout the year and are gunning for a promotion. However, only Tom gets to move up the corporate ladder in the next appraisal. Assuming they had all followed the rules of "fair play," then Tom had no influence on the final decision. Several factors, like leadership skills, a growth mindset, etc., could have influenced the management's choice. In this situation, if Tom feels guilty, then it reflects unreasonable guilt.

In the case of reasonable guilt, you can strive to make amends to the extent possible. Even a heartfelt "sorry" does the trick more often than not. Once you have taken remedial action, you can't continue to blame yourself. Allow yourself to heal.

For unreasonable guilt, rationalise with yourself that you have not manipulated the outcome, and hence, you are not at fault. As an added act of compassion, you can try to guide your friends to prepare for the hurdles to the best of their abilities.

I lost my father when I was just 21. The financial situation felt like the world was crumbling beneath my feet. While I managed to steady the ship and come out of life's most unexpected challenge pretty much unscathed,

I kept missing my father every day for years. I wasn't missing his advice or company; what was it that I was missing? Or what was it that made me wake up sweating in the middle of the night?

I realised after deep introspection that what kept bothering me the most was the feeling that I didn't react on time when he was having a stroke. "If only you had taken action immediately…" my mind would sneer at me every now and then.

Gradually, I convinced myself that it was an irreversible situation. I couldn't have done more than I did. My initial reaction was also not unjust in the given circumstances.

After 21 years, the vacuum is still there, and the feeling of not reacting on time hasn't vanished either, but I'm able to cope with the memories a lot better than I did in the initial 3–4 years of the incident.

The grumbling grudges

COVID-19 has been a life-transforming experience, even for those who have been spared the deadly viral attack. Many of us have accumulated a lot of mental garbage that we have not been able to dispose of efficiently. This is where the concept of "letting go" steps in.

In recent years, with my increased interest in the power of the mind and its amazing potency, I've explored numerous techniques to let go of past grudges, guilt, and associated negative feelings.

After experimenting with various approaches, I discovered that the simple philosophy of acceptance works best for me. The thoughts may still linger in your mind, but over a period of time, they will stop bothering you as much.

Instead, if you are overly intense in uprooting the emotions, you may end up inviting more acute feelings that are harder to deal with.

Image by Motoki Tonn (Unsplash)

Be aware, but not judgemental

The mind is a battlefield of thoughts. While the internet dishes out figures of 6,000 to 70,000 thoughts a day, the numbers are staggering anyway. If we add the probabilities of 80% negative and 95% repetitive thoughts, then the game becomes even more complex. Can you completely let go of all your bad thoughts and feelings without starting a new battle in your mind?

Mindfulness is an easy-to-adopt approach that allows you to handle negative emotions in a rational manner. As you draw your attention to your breath in the silence of a meditative atmosphere, your thoughts continue to come and go. But with practice, you can cultivate the mind to just observe the thoughts and let them pass.

Take the route of acceptance, cognisance, and learning. Accept the unalterable nature of the incident, be aware of the emotions it triggers, and try to filter out any learning from the occurrence.

Eventually, you may manage to heal yourself completely from the unpleasant experience: a gradual manifestation of the art of "letting go!"

IT'S ALL IN THE BALANCE, OR IS IT?

FINDING THE PERFECT EQUILIBRIUM

Work-Life Balance – A perennial illusion or a tangible reality?

Image by Gustavo Torres (unsplash)

Where to find the balance of life?

Words or phrases like "stress," "burnout," "marital disharmony," etc., have become harsh realities of modern life. As we seek the Midas touch that will turn our woes into an abundance of joy, work-life balance keeps coming up as an answer to our internal and external problems.

Is it a modern-day phenomenon? Or has the concept of a balanced life been around for ages? To find the answers, let us take a closer look at some of the holy scriptures of the world that are treasure troves of wisdom relevant in this day and age.

The teachings of the Holy Bible

Ecclesiastes 3:1–8: "For everything there is a season, and a time for every matter under heaven: ...... a time to embrace and a time to refrain from embracing...."

John 9:4 says, "We must work the works for him who sent me, while it is day; night comes, when no one can work."

Colossians 3:23–24 says, "Whatever your task, work heartily, as serving the Lord and not men."

These messages from the Holy Book of Christianity emphasise the significance of work-life balance. While our devotion to work should be unflinching, we should also set out the time for work judiciously.

The Islamic Perspective

Mohammed Faris is the founder of The Productive Muslim Company and an international coach, author, and speaker. He draws inferences from the holy book of Islam to show how the Prophet led us to a "total life balance" that keeps the essence of putting 100% of your attention on work and your personal life while doing each activity.

Lessons from the Bhagavad Gita

Lesson 1 (Karma Yoga)

Karmanyevadhikaraste ma phalesu kadacana

Ma karmaphalaheturbhurma te sango'stvakarmani (II:47)

This verse says that we have a choice over our actions, but not over the results of those actions. Do not be attached to the results; however, this doesn't imply that we should choose inaction.

To give this message a modern perspective, if we focus less on the results of our work, it will give us peace and control over the hard work we do, which is a must for a satisfying career. Enjoy the process, and let the results follow on their own.

In a concert, a musician becomes immersed in his own melodies; the applause that follows or the cheque he receives from the organisers are obvious byproducts of his dedication to his art.

Lesson 2 (Sankhya Yoga)

Yoga Karmasu Kaushalam (2.50)

We should work hard and to the best of our abilities, but we shouldn't waste time. Instead, we should be efficient enough to finish the job on time.

Let's think about how, in some modern societies, working long hours has become the norm in the business world. But have we considered how much our habits contribute to this situation?

Think of the many times when we lose focus, like when we take extra coffee breaks, waste time on social media, or talk with coworkers about other people. If the time was used to complete the work for the day, chances are that we could have headed home early.

Of course, this doesn't factor in the random, last-minute assignments; more on that later.

Let us now divert our attention to relatively modern times.

Image by Museums Victoria (unsplash)

Industrial Revolutions in Britain and America

From 1760 to 1840, Britain shifted its focus from farming to a manufacturing-centric economy. Factories and workshops started cropping up in great numbers. The factory owners were keen to maximise the operational hours of the workers; thus, the labourers worked for 14–16 hours a day, six days a week.

After the Civil War (1861–1865), the social and economic structure of the United States changed in a big way. The 1890s witnessed massive industrial growth, which meant long working hours for the labourers; they often stretched beyond 10 or 12 hours a day.

If we analyse these two periods, "work-life balance" seems a far cry. However, the situation did call for a single-minded focus on economic growth, so supporters of these revolutions may be able to justify the need for long work hours.

In 1920, Henry Ford made the "9 to 5" work culture the new normal in the United States. However, Welsh manufacturer and activist Robert Owen, known as the "Father of British Socialism," had earlier popularised the concept. Owen coined the phrase "8 hours labour, 8 hours recreation, and 8 hours rest" in 1817.

Owen's interest in European textile mills had faded by 1829, so his son, Robert Dale Owen, made the decision to move the business to the United States. Inspired by Owen's ideologies, the labour movement gained impetus in the USA. Their efforts finally reaped rich dividends in 1898, when the United Mine Workers won an 8-hour-a-day work shift. Eventually, Ford and other manufacturing companies in the country started following the same routine that got embedded in US law in 1940 and gradually became accepted worldwide.

As time went by, people realised that without adequate family and personal time, their productivity was also diminishing. Hugo Munsterberg, a German psychologist, wrote in his book "Psychology and Industrial Efficiency" that cutting the workday from 9 to 8 hours can actually make people more productive, not less.

Impact of technology, consumerism, and globalisation on work-life balance

The digital revolution has transformed the way industries operate. It has the inherent quality of reducing the turnaround time, thus augmenting production efficiency. However, what we witness is increased engagement with work beyond conventional working hours. In 1972, Ray Tomlinson discovered the @ symbol on the keyboard, and email, as we know it today, was born.

Since then, emails, chat apps, video conferencing, and other technologies have quietly crept into our personal lives. In our quest to be "on top of our work," we are ready to sacrifice our dinner times, sleep, weekends, and even vacations.

So what is this near-crazy devotion to our careers all about? Is it another Klondike gold rush in Yukon, Canada, ala the famous Charles Chaplin movie? Or is it the impact of consumerism?

Edward Diener, a PhD and researcher of subjective well-being and materialism at the University of Illinois, thinks that chasing material wealth will have an impact on our social lives. Knox College psychologist Tim Kasser mentions that people who build their life goals on strong materialistic values are likely to have poorer well-being.

Globalisation has further fuelled the urge to own expensive materials that our cousins in Western countries may possess. If a childhood friend from India has shifted to the US and has the latest iPad, we may be tempted to buy one immediately.

This frantic search for the best things in the world can take us away from what we really want. Will the exotic vacation be so memorable if our beloved partners are not there to savour the moment? Should we shower our children with high-end gadgets or give them the best education that we can afford?

Take a moment to ponder over these questions before you read further…

Why is this balance so important?

If we take into account the four Ashramas of Hinduism—Brahmacharya, Grihastha, Vanaprastha, and Sannyasa—we would see that we play specific roles in every stage of our lives that are subject to societal and natural laws.

In today's world, the last two stages hardly exist, which makes the first two even more significant. During our time as students (Brahmacharya), we need to find enough time to study, but we should also spend quality time on our hobbies, with friends and family, and getting ready for the onward journey.

As we move into the Grihastha phase (family life), our responsibilities grow, but if we make good use of the Brahmacharya stage, we'll be ready for the challenges. Here, we have to realise that this is the time to enjoy "Kama" (our desires) while making sure we earn enough "Artha" (wealth) to meet our family's material needs.

Taking a cue from the above discourse, let's build the foundation for a balanced life that gives us time for both work and family.

Image by National Cancer Institute (unsplash)

5-step mantra for work-life balance

Find your Ikigai

Ikigai is a Japanese concept that revolves around finding your niche in the world. It tells you to base your career on one of your main interests, which can also be a meaningful way to make a living.

Imagine building a career in digital art if you have had the experience of painting since childhood. It could be just the vocation you were meant to follow. The field also offers immense commercial potential to earn you a healthy livelihood.

In his best-selling book "Winning," Jack Welch, the well-known former CEO of General Electric Company, shares important lessons for the business world, especially for younger people. The third lesson is, in essence, "Keep trying different jobs till you find the one you love," Welch professes that, contrary to widely held HR beliefs, there is no harm in changing jobs until you find your niche, whether within or outside the organization. Once you do that, you will be at your most productive.

Plan your day in advance

Remember the mystical sages of Sivana in the Robin Sharma bestseller, "The Monk Who Sold His Ferrari?" By internalizing the message conveyed in this masterpiece, you can start noting down the main activities that you must complete the following day. You can do the same for your weekly tasks on Sunday evenings. This way, you are sure to avoid any loss of time, which is of the essence.

Not just managing your time, but mastering it, will allow you to enjoy your personal life without jeopardizing your job responsibilities.

De-stress

The demanding nature of our professional pursuits and our household responsibilities may have an impact on our mental health.

Take time out for meditation and exercise. Even if you are able to inculcate this regime for 15–20 minutes a day, you will be much better prepared for the tasks that lie ahead.

De-stressing has many important health and social benefits, such as better sleep, better weight management, less muscle tension, a better mood, and a happier family life.

We-time

The digital invasion has robbed us of valuable family time. Though watching a movie together is also fun, you can instead play a game of puzzles or carom.

Puzzles are good for your health in many ways, and they also make your home a fun place to be.

If you are experiencing any communication gaps or disturbances in the family, the following routine can bring amazing changes to your family ties:

- Make a conscious effort to have dinner at the designated dinner table instead of on the couch.
- Keep your mobile phones off, if possible. If you have to keep them on, then try putting them on vibration and flipping them over so that you don't see the screen flashing with incessant social media updates.
- Engage in household chores or gardening over the weekend as a family.
- Involve the kids in preparing a fun meal for the Sunday brunch.
- Keep a family reading time where one member can read out interesting (not gory, please) news or a section of a book. The entire family can discuss the issue by sharing their own perspective.

Learn to say "no" at work

Just when you are about to leave for home, the boss shoves another tedious job on your shoulder. In this rat race, we often take on these extra responsibilities to speed up our careers, but we end up being disappointed with the results.

Find a polite way to say no to unsolicited extra work. Instead, use this time to upgrade your skills by learning something relevant to your field of work. Your enhanced knowledge and new skillsets will win you more professional accolades than being a "yes man" to your superior would.

Happiness lies in finding a suitable (if not perfect) work-life balance that takes care of your priorities. While it may seem daunting or even outright unrealistic to some people, it's worth giving it a shot. Once you start reaping the long-term benefits of a balanced life, you will realise that it's worth the effort.

Stay healthy, happy, and blessed!

SUCCESS IS A JOURNEY, NOT A DESTINATION

CHASING THE ULTIMATE DESTINATION

Are you inspired by the 7-figure or the million-dollar success stories? Or, are they pushing you back into your shell? Let's look at success from a new lens…

Image by Freepik

When you make a career transition or embark on a new life journey, there's a plethora of emotions that engulf you.

One moment, you are apprehensive about the uncertainties that lie ahead.

Another moment, you are excited about the same unpredictable future that beckons you.

Amidst all these surges of contradictory or complementary emotions, what propels you onward is a dream of a successful life.

While the definition of 'success' will vary from person to person, in the material world, some elements of materialistic success are bound to enter your thoughts.

And, of course, there's nothing wrong with aspiring to become rich. Your success in the world might even inspire you to engage in many charitable or spiritual endeavours.

However, the path to your desired goals could be riddled with hindrances.

Stumbling, falling, rising, and falling again, only to push yourself one more time toward that dream destination… it's never a bed of roses.

Yet, this roller-coaster ride is so intrinsic to the rewards that you receive in the end.

Hence, the questions that I ask are:

> *"Do you call yourself successful only when you have millions in assets?"*
>
> *"Isn't the road to success a mark of success itself?"*

About three years ago, circumstances pushed me to answer my calling and start a new journey as a writer.

🚀 I dreamed that my first step into the realm of professional writing would be a blockbuster beginning- My book, "Fakeism," appreciated by those who read, didn't quite make me the next J.K. Rowling (or Robin Sharma, as it's a creative nonfiction). 😁

🚀 I was excited to get a break in the next couple of months in the growing online content-writing industry. Did my struggles end with this? Far from it, as I kept fighting to scale up and find a stronger foothold in the market. 😁

🚀 Have I been able to break the jinx and enter the high-paying markets yet? Not, really. I'm still trying to stay afloat. 😁

Then, what the heck makes me feel 'successful?'

Well, I have done the following in the process:

⭐ I successfully overcame my fear of publishing my book (and eventually writing on Medium.com).

⭐ I successfully managed to find regular work (albeit at low-moderate rates) in a competitive market, scaling up gradually but surely.

⭐ I successfully upgraded my skills, and I'm still continuing to do so.

⭐ I successfully keep negative thoughts of failure at bay, as I know the path that I've chosen will lead me to the material success that I deserve.

Am I being bullheaded? Maybe, yes.

But have I stopped taking a rational approach toward my goals? No, I have enrolled in relevant courses with proven track records, I've subscribed to newsletters of highly successful writers who share great tips, and I have taken steps to improve my outreach to potential clients.

There is still a lot more to do. But I'm on my way to realising my goals.

That's success for me.

When the millions start pouring, I'll pop the champagne and celebrate this 'successful' journey.

Let all the rags-to-riches stories inspire you in your journey, wherever you are. However, the real learning is in the process that those people share, not the end results.

As mentioned in Colossians 3:23-24, "Whatever you do, work at it with all your heart, as working for the Lord, not for human masters, since you know that you will receive an inheritance from the Lord as a reward. It is the Lord Christ you are serving."